SRA ART Connections

Artist Profiles

Columbus, OH

The **McGraw·Hill** Companies

Photo Credits

SRAonline.com

 SRA

Send all inquiries to:
SRA/McGraw-Hill
8787 Orion Place
Columbus, OH 43240-4027

Printed in the United States of America.

ISBN 0-07-601838-5

1 2 3 4 5 6 7 8 9 DBH 08 07 06 05 04

The McGraw-Hill Companies

Table of Contents

Ansel Adams
1902–1984

Ansel Adams (an´ səl ad´ əms) was born in San Francisco. In 1903, his family moved to a house amid the sand dunes near the ocean. Adams always believed that the sights, sounds, and smells of the ocean shaped the way he thought. Adams had a difficult time at school. With his father's approval, he quit early, intending to become a classical pianist. He became fascinated with the beauty of places such as the Yosemite valley, but was frustrated that his photography did not catch its inherent grandeur. As he pursued perfecting his photographic and development processes his talent became evident to others, and books containing his photographs began to sell. His popularity continued to increase, even after his death in 1984.

▲ **Ansel Adams.** (American). *Self-Portrait.*

Silver gelatin print.

About Art History

Georgia O'Keeffe's husband, Alfred Stieglitz, had a small gallery in New York City called An American Place. He gave Adams a show of his own in 1936. Stieglitz was an important advocate for both O'Keeffe and Adams. He also displayed the photography of Paul Strand and the paintings of John Marin.

About the Artwork

Adams wanted to share his appreciation of nature through his photography. He was a member of the Sierra Club and worked for that organization toward the preservation and appreciation of natural resources. Adams constantly experimented with materials and techniques to create the finest prints possible. He printed his photograph *Moonrise, Hernandez,* taken in 1941, more than 1,300 times, and finally felt he got it right in the 1970s.

About the Media

Adams began taking photographs on a Kodak Box Brownie camera in 1916. He tried many cameras over the years, even an instant Polaroid. He did some work with color in the mid-1940s, but because color photographs fade over time, he preferred to work in black and white.

About the Technique

Before he took a photograph, Adams visualized the scene, recorded the camera settings, and took notes about the process. Adams felt that his darkroom ability was as important as his photographic ability. He made gelatin silver prints, which are papers coated with gelatin that contains light-sensitive silver salts. They were developed in the 1870s and had the advantage of not turning yellow and being simpler to produce. Gelatin silver prints remain the standard black-and-white print type.

▲ **Noland Anderson.** (American).
Blue Dome-House Blessing. 1955.

Stained and etched glass. 17 inches (43.18 cm.) diameter.
Private collection.

Noland Anderson

b. 1969

Noland Anderson (nô´ land an´ dər sən) was born in Virginia in 1969. He studied art formally at the Fort Lauderdale School of Fine Arts in Florida. Although he works primarily in watercolors, Anderson also draws with pencil as a court artist. When a court proceeding is closed to cameras and video crews, court artists create drawings of the trial and its participants to be shown on television and in newspapers. Court artists must be able to sketch quickly and accurately in line and color. The images of people involved in court cases must be recognizable to the public. These artists often work on a freelance basis, being called in to draw courtroom proceedings when the need arises. Currently Anderson works and lives in Miami, Florida.

About Art History

Blue Dome-House Blessing can be classified as an illumination. Historically illuminations were the colorful illustrations, usually accented with gold leaf, alongside text in ancient manuscripts. During the Middle Ages in Europe the practice of creating illuminations on the handwritten pages of texts became a specialized art form. Some illumination artists concentrated their talents in one aspect of manuscript illustration, such as creating elaborate page borders or applying gold leaf with incredibly detailed precision. The skill with which Anderson painted his *Blue Dome-House Blessing* is evident in the beautiful composition, fine detail, brilliant colors, and deftly applied gold leaf.

About the Artwork

Blue Dome-House Blessing is patterned after the huge, spectacular stained-glass dome in the main synagogue of Szeged, Hungary. The synagogue, completed in 1903, is an enormous building with its length and width extending to the size of one entire city block. The stained-glass dome measures ten meters in diameter. Anderson's painting is a much more diminutive 17 square inches.

About the Media

Blue Dome-House Blessing was created in stained and etched glass. The colors include vibrant shades of blue, and gold embossing has been added to give a luminous quality.

Sofonisba Anguissola
1532-1625

Sofonisba Anguissola (sō fō nēz´ ba ang gwō´ shō lä) was born in 1532 in the northern Italian city of Cremona. Her family encouraged her and her five sisters to take art lessons and to be creative. They were so talented that travelers would go out of their way to visit the family. Anguissola's father arranged for her to travel to Rome to study with Michelangelo, who was the best living artist in Italy. In 1559, Anguissola was invited to become the court painter of King Philip II of Spain. She remained at the court for 20 years. Her professional career as a painter ended when she married in 1569, but she continued to paint for the rest of her life.

▲ **Sofonisba Anguissola.** (Italian). *Self Portrait, Painting the Madonna (detail).* 1556.

Oil on canvas. 66 × 57 cm. Museum Zamek, Lancucie, Lancut, Poland.

About Art History

Anguissola was the first professional female Italian painter. She painted realistic pictures, and was influenced by Michelangelo and the regional painters of Cremona. She was a role model for other Italian women who wanted to become artists. Lavina Fontana, Fede Galizia, and other women from northern Italy followed her example and became artists in the late sixteenth century. More than 50 of Anguissola's paintings have been saved. This is a large number of works for a woman of this period.

About the Artwork

Anguissola usually painted portraits. Before moving to Spain she painted portraits of her family. In Spain, she painted portraits for the royal family. In some of her paintings people appear to be talking to each other. These paintings were known as *conversation pieces.* This style of painting gained popularity after Anguissola introduced it in Italy. Anguissola painted more self-portraits than most artists of her time.

About the Media

Anguissola usually painted on canvas with oil paints. She prepared her own painting materials, as did all artists at that time.

About the Technique

Anguissola is known for being able to convey emotions through the facial expressions she painted. She was famous for introducing smiles and laughter into portrait painting.

Jennifer Bartlett

b. 1941

Jennifer Bartlett (jen´ ə fər bärt´ let) is an installation artist, painter, printmaker, and sculptor. She was born in Long Beach, California, and studied at Mills College and the Yale School of Art and Architecture. Yale's progressive teaching approach influenced Bartlett's early artwork in the 1960s and 1970s, and she has experimented with concepts and materials throughout her artistic career.

About Art History

While studying art Bartlett was exposed to many different styles and media, especially the large, expressive paintings of Joan Mitchell and Adolph Gottlieb. Influences of pointillism, impressionism and expressionism can be seen in her work, as well as the influence of Henri Matisse, Pablo Picasso, Jasper Johns, and Jackson Pollock. Bartlett has participated in exhibitions and created public commissions throughout the country and abroad since the 1980s.

About the Artwork

Themes of variation and repetition often appear in Bartlett's work, and she has made a number of paintings that use multiple perspectives, as in her *Air* Series. She also focuses on grid-based interpretations of environmental subjects such as her piece *Rhapsody,* an installation consisting of 988 steel plates painted with landscape imagery and covered with grids. Houses, trees, and water

are frequently included in her work as seen in the print *Swimmer Lost at Night (for Tom Hess).* In addition to recognizable and tangible subjects, Bartlett is well-known for her abstract, colorful, plaid patterns that seem to move across the canvas.

About the Media

Bartlett works in brush and ink, oils, pastels, and gouache. She paints on canvas and sometimes on paper.

About the Technique

Bartlett's artwork incorporates both abstraction and realism. At times she creates *minimalist* art, depicting images and subjects in a simple manner without extravagant detail.

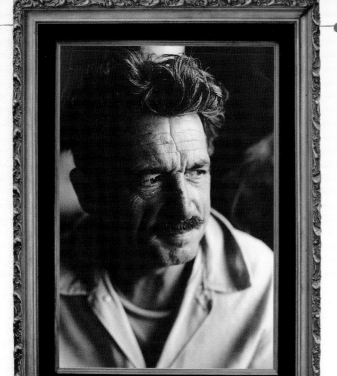

Thomas Hart Benton
1889-1975

Thomas Hart Benton (tom´ əs hart bent´ ən) was a regional American painter known for his energetic, colorful murals. He was the son of a United States congressional representative and named after his great uncle, a famous pre-American Civil War senator. From his family, Benton developed a strong identity as an American. He studied art in Paris and at the Art Institute of Chicago. Benton believed that American artists should develop their own styles and not just copy French painting styles. Although Benton began his art career as a cartoonist, he was known for his murals depicting scenes from the rural past of the American Midwest.

About Art History

Benton painted subjects from mostly one region —the American Midwest. He helped develop and promote the American art style known as *regionalism.* He urged American artists to paint scenes from the lives of ordinary Americans. He also encouraged his students to try new ideas in their work. One of his students was the famous painter Jackson Pollock.

About the Artwork

Benton enjoyed painting Midwestern farm scenes. Many of his paintings show sunburned farmers and huge work horses. In *Cradling Wheat,* several farmers and one of their sons are shown harvesting wheat by hand. Benton's paintings remind viewers of days gone by in rural America.

About the Media

Along with other media, Benton used oil and egg tempera.

About the Technique

Benton used his experience as a cartoonist in his later paintings by dividing scenes with borders, like a comic strip.

Isabel Bishop
1902-1988

Isabel Bishop (iz´ a bel bish´ əp) was born in Cincinnati, Ohio. A year later, her family moved to a run-down neighborhood in Detroit, Michigan, where her father was employed as the principal of a nearby high school. Her parents didn't think the neighborhood children made good playmates, so Bishop spent much of her time alone. She graduated from high school at age 15 and then studied art. She moved to New York City, where she continued to study art and began exhibiting her work. She loved to paint the people in Union Square.

Bishop married in 1934, moved to the suburbs, and had a son. She commuted to her studio on the Square every day for 40 years. Looking down from her studio in an office building, she watched the people below as she worked. During her life, Bishop won many awards and honors. Her paintings hang in museums across the nation.

About Art History

Bishop's style was influenced by the Baroque period and especially the work of Peter Paul Rubens. She liked the way he used layers of washes as an underpainting and then added glazes over the painting to create a sense of movement. Bishop's early work was "real beyond reality." It gradually gained an abstract cubist quality as she began to emphasize the patterns she saw in the architecture, colors, and shadows of Union Square.

About the Artwork

Bishop created paintings, drawings, and prints. She is best known for her pictures of Union Square, such as *On the Street.* Sometimes called an "urban realist," she painted the shoppers and workers in the square.

About the Media

Bishop painted in oils over tempera and created etchings in aquatint.

About the Technique

Toward the end of her career, Bishop added transparent veils of color and networks of dots and lines to her paintings. She portrayed people as nearly transparent; they seemed to be moving in a mist, contributing to the overall abstract quality.

Fernando Botero
b. 1932

As a young man, this Colombian spent two years learning to be a matador. Fernando Botero (fer nän´ dō bōtä´ rō) changed his career plans and studied art in Colombia, Spain, France, and Italy. During this time, Botero had several exhibitions, but received little praise for his work—and fewer sales. After he began painting in a rounded style in 1956, his pictures sold well. By 1958, he was Colombia's most famous young artist. In 1960, he opened a studio in New York City. In 1973, he moved to Paris and began sculpting. He has married twice and has four children.

About Art History

In his early years, Botero was influenced by modern French and Spanish painters, along with the Renaissance masters. At one time he was expelled from a conservative art school for praising Picasso. In time, he settled on his own style, which features rounded figures.

About the Artwork

Botero draws portraits of individuals and groups. Much of his work shows the influence of his South American background, such as its food, music, religion, and architecture. Some characters appear again and again in his work, such as a Colombian man with a thin mustache. His sculptures range from human figures and animals to a giant coffeepot. Many pieces have the same rounded shapes he uses in his drawings. Some of Botero's work is serious and some is playful.

About the Media

Botero expresses his ideas in oils, pencil and charcoal drawings, watercolors, and bronze and marble sculptures.

About the Technique

Botero sometimes does quick sketches before beginning an oil painting. Many of his drawings, however, are finished works of art. He completes some in charcoal on canvas, such as *A Family*. For other drawings, he uses a thick pencil but no shading. When sculpting, Botero begins by making a sketch or a clay model. Then a workshop produces a plaster model for him, and Botero decides whether to have technicians carve the finished product in marble or cast it in bronze.

William Adolphe Bouguereau
1825–1905

Born on the west coast of France, William Adolphe Bouguereau (wēl´ yəm a dôlf´ boo´ grō´) grew up in a family with little money. He put himself through art school with money he earned from painting portraits, and soon was regarded as one of the best classical painters of his time. His strong work ethic was constant throughout his career, and he was known and respected for his compassion for other struggling artists. In 1883, he became president of the Society of Painters, Architects, Sculptors, Engravers, and Designers, an establishment that promoted and aided new and struggling artists. His classical style was often challenged by progressive artists, but he became one of France's most respected artists.

About Art History

While Bouguereau was painting highly realistic and classical compositions his contemporaries were involved with the growing impressionist movement. This new style of Renoir, Pissarro, and Cassat was a rebellion against Bouguereau's academic style influenced by Jaques-Louis David and Jean-Auguste-Dominic Ingres. His subjects included classical, mythological, and allegorical themes and often included links to contemporary history. As his career gained official and public acclaim Bouguereau was awarded the Grand Medal of Honour at the 1885 Salon.

About the Artwork

Bouguereau's work celebrates the idealism of scenes in everyday life. Bathers, children, mothers, and religious compositions were predominant among his subjects, and his conservative artistic style valued strict rules of anatomy, perspective, and academic modeling. In *The Nut Gatherers* he created a scene of innocence between two young girls still unaware of the dangers of life. They have bare feet and fresh faces which remind the viewer of simple pleasures and youthful friendship.

About the Media

Bouguereau painted in oils on canvas and was a great proponent of a dedicated study of contour and the classical figure. He was very close to his mother and created a number of mother and child paintings. These were thought to reference his love for his own mother as well as the more obvious Madonna and Child compositions. His industrious and dedicated nature allowed him to complete more than seven hundred paintings in his lifetime.

About the Technique

The dedication with which Bouguereau worked filtered into all aspects of his creative life. Not only did he believe in constant practice and study of classical form and technique, he also researched and studied his subjects in numerous sketches before creating finished paintings.

Georges Braque
1882-1963

Georges Braque (zhorzh brak) was born in Argenteuil-sur-Seine, France. Helping his father, a house decorator, taught him much about painting. In 1900 he moved to Paris to study under a master decorator. He then spent several years painting at the Académie Humbert. Braque worked with Pablo Picasso in creating cubism, but after fighting in World War I, he ended his work with Picasso. His style constantly evolved until his death in 1963.

About Art History

Braque began painting in the impressionist style, but soon was attracted to fauvism—a style whose name comes from a French word for "wild beasts." Fauvists, such as Henri Matisse, tended to use colors in an intense and violent way. Braque's style took another turn when he met Pablo Picasso and saw his *Les Demoiselles d'Avignon.* Together Braque and Picasso worked to develop cubism, a style that shows the world from a number of different viewpoints.

About the Artwork

After meeting Picasso, Braque began to paint stark, abstract landscapes of geometric forms. As Braque and Picasso developed the cubist style, Braque began to incorporate collage into his paintings. His most abstract works of art during this time were filled with gray, brown, and black broken forms.

After 1917 Braque's work combined cubism with decorative, sensual elements, and by the end of his life he painted nature in a more realistic way.

About the Media

Braque was the first cubist to incorporate collages of pasted paper into his paintings. In addition to paintings, Braque created lithographs, sculptures, stained-glass windows, and jewelry designs. He also designed the sets for two ballets.

About the Technique

Braque and Picasso went through several developmental phases of cubism. During one of these phases, Braque tried to reduce natural forms to basic geometric shapes and show them on a two-dimensional plane. He glued bits of paper, sand, and sawdust into some of his paintings to create texture.

Frederick Brosen

b. 1954

Frederick Brosen (fre´drik brō´ sən) was born and raised in New York and continues to work there today. He is regarded as one of America's leading contemporary watercolor artists and has received great acclaim for his realistic depictions of urban landscapes, particularly street scenes. Brosen studied at City College of New York, the Art Students League, and Pratt Institute, and has been exhibiting around the country since the early 1980s, earning recognition for his watercolors and lithography. Brosen is now the instructor of watercolor at the National Academy School of Fine Arts in New York.

About Art History

After he graduated with an M.F.A. from Pratt Institute in 1979, Brosen continued working with watercolors. He established his reputation at his first exhibition in 1982. He has participated in numerous group and solo shows, and has taught at both Dartmouth College and Woodmere Academy.

About the Artwork

The acute detail and realism of Brosen's style characterize his work. Views of parks, street corners, and bridges are found in his compositions. Brosen intentionally leaves images of people out of his paintings, allowing the viewer to concentrate on the urban-landscape subject. Brosen emphasizes the age and color gradation of buildings and architectural structures, which draws attention to the city as an historical place.

About the Media

Brosen works in watercolor.

About the Technique

Brosen first sketches a scene, photographs it, and then sketches it a second time. This thorough method takes time, but once he is satisfied with his preliminary studies he lightly draws the final composition on watercolor paper. He then applies watercolors in light washes and many layers, building the color intensity with each layer.

Roger Brown
1941-1997

Roger Brown (roj´ ər broun) was born in Hamilton, Alabama. He moved to Chicago when he was 21 and studied for several years at the Art Institute of Chicago. He received his master's degree in fine arts in 1970. His art has been shown in many museums around the United States. Even though he lived and worked in Chicago, Brown liked to paint scenes of different regions of the country. The primary focus of his art was the land and people of the United States.

About Art History

The Chicago Imagists are a group of artists from Chicago who paint landscapes with few people and simple colors. Many of these artists, like Brown, paint expressive pictures that reflect how the artist feels. Many of Brown's paintings look like fantastic cartoons. Objects in his work are often stylized. Their smooth, repeating shapes make patterns across the surface of the canvas.

About the Artwork

Brown painted pictures of many regions of the United States. He painted rural landscapes as well as city scenes. The people in his paintings are usually just dark shadows in the shape of a person.

About the Media

Brown generally worked in oils on canvas.

About the Technique

Brown usually painted his landscapes by putting the horizon line high in the picture. As a result, the viewer gets the sense of looking at his paintings from high above the ground. Then Brown drew in the people and buildings with simple shapes and colored them with solid colors. Sometimes he painted strange colors or designs on the ground or in the sky. From a distance, the surfaces of many of his paintings look patterned. Brown also used different scales in the same painting. For example, he made people inside buildings look larger or smaller than life-size.

Elizabeth Catlett

b. 1915

Elizabeth Catlett (ə liz´ ə bəth kat´ lət) was born into a comfortable African American family in Washington, D.C. She went to public school there and later attended Howard University, where she graduated with honors. She also earned her master of fine arts degree from the State University of Iowa, where she studied under Grant Wood. During the 1940s, Catlett used mother-and-child themes in her realistic sculptures. During the next ten years she moved toward abstraction, generating smooth rounded forms and graceful elongated figures. During the 1960s and 1970s, she created expressionistic sculptures and prints showing African and militant themes. Catlett became a citizen of Mexico in 1962. She married the Mexican artist Francisco Mora and is celebrated as one of Mexico's greatest artists.

About Art History

Catlett studied with James Potter and James Wells at Howard University. After she saw the artwork of muralist Diego Rivera, she changed her major from design to painting.

About the Artwork

Catlett chooses African American people for her subjects—most frequently women who struggle to maintain family and community. Her work is highly expressionistic and emotional.

About the Media

Catlett has produced a number of stone sculptures, paintings, and lithographs, as well as linoleum prints in black and white and color.

About the Technique

Catlett's works always appear as strong statements of the life of African Americans. Her work shows soft, moving surfaces and little embellishment. She polishes her stone sculptures to a shiny, slick smoothness.

▲ **George Catlin.** (American). *NO-HO-MUN-YA, One Who Gives No Attention.* 1844.

Oil on canvas. 29 × 24 inches (73.66 × 60.96 cm.).
Smithsonian American Art Museum, Washington, D.C.

George Catlin
1796–1872

George Catlin (jorj kat´ lən) was born in Pennsylvania. He first became a lawyer, but painting lured him away from a law career. While painting miniatures in Philadelphia, he happened to meet a visiting group of Native Americans, and Catlin became fascinated by Native American culture. He made many trips into Native American territory and spent weeks studying groups that had not yet been influenced by European culture. He spent his own money to exhibit his paintings in England and France, where they were much admired. Living on a small income, Catlin traveled to South America to paint genre paintings of indigenous groups. Catlin has had more paintings displayed in the Louvre in Paris, France, than any other American artist.

About Art History

Catlin was the first artist to devote his entire career to painting genre paintings of Native Americans. His paintings are considered the most complete record of native groups in North and South America between 1830 and 1860. He insisted that no one could accurately paint these groups without living among them. Today, many Native Americans rely on his images for information about costumes and traditions of the past.

About the Artwork

Catlin eschewed stereotypical representations of Native Americans and created portraits showing their individuality. Examples include *Man Who Tracks* and *Red Jacket.* Catlin also painted Native American ceremonies, such as *Sioux Dog Feast,* and landscapes, such as *Buffaloes in the Salt Meadows.* Catlin created more than 500 paintings and wrote several books about Native American customs and ceremonies. He tried to sell his paintings to the United States government, but was unsuccessful.

About the Media

Catlin worked in both watercolors and oils.

About the Technique

Catlin thought of himself as a wilderness painter, not a studio painter. He often made quick, outdoor graphite or watercolor sketches before painting in oils in his studio. Catlin tried to depict his subject matter in the most realistic and accurate fashion possible.

▲ **Paul Cézanne.** (French). *Self Portrait with Hat.*
c. 1879

Oil on canvas. 44½ × 33 inches (113 × 84 cm.)
Kunstmuseum, Bern, Switzerland.

Paul Cézanne
1839–1906

Paul Cézanne (paul sā zan´) was born in the south of France in Aix-en-Provence. He is often called the father of modern art. He loved to paint, but people did not like his work much—at least not during his lifetime. He had to beg gallery owners to show his work, and therefore he did not sell many paintings. He inherited money from his parents to pay his bills and buy his paints. He continued painting until a week before he died.

About Art History

Cézanne was a postimpressionist. He was greatly influenced by the painter Camille Pissarro. Pissarro introduced Cézanne to the new impressionist technique for capturing outdoor light. Cézanne combined impressionism with a formal instruction the impressionists had abandoned. He looked closely at things to find their basic forms and shapes. Cézanne painted cylinders, spheres, and cones to show these forms. Sometimes he changed the shapes he saw in nature to make his paintings more interesting. Picasso, Matisse, and other artists studied Cézanne's ideas.

About the Artwork

Cézanne painted landscapes, still lifes, and portraits. Many of his landscapes were of the countryside and mountains near his home. He developed a unique way of representing nature and objects in a highly creative and abstract fashion. Cézanne painted slowly, often taking several days to create a still life. One friend posed 115 times so Cézanne could finish his portrait.

About the Media

Cézanne worked in both oils and watercolors.

About the Technique

Cézanne used bright colors and bold brushstrokes, especially in the skies of his landscapes. He applied the paint in vertical and horizontal lines. He knew that cool colors seem to pull back and warm colors seem to go forward. Cézanne also used different shades of the same color to add shape to his subjects. His knowledge made his paintings seem three-dimensional.

Marc Chagall
1887–1985

Marc Chagall (mark sha gäl′) was born in a small town in Russia, Vitebsk, which is now part of Belarus. He studied art in Saint Petersburg and then in Paris, France. After the Russian revolution he served as the director of the art academy in his hometown. From 1919 to 1922, Chagall was the art director of the Moscow Jewish State Theater. He painted murals in the theater lobby and created sets for the shows. In 1923, he moved to France. He spent most of the rest of his life there, except for a brief period of residence in the United States from 1941 to 1948.

About Art History

Chagall was one of the first people to paint pictures that looked like dreams. For example, he created many paintings of animals and people flying through the air, sometimes upside down. Chagall is sometimes referred to as an early surrealist because of his dreamlike style and the element of fantasy in his work.

About the Artwork

Born into a very religious Jewish family, Chagall's work shows the strong influence of his home and his heritage. He included childhood memories and religious images in his work. His work combines memories with folklore and fantasy. Chagall created 12 stained-glass windows for the Hadassah Hospital in Jerusalem, Israel, illustrating the Old Testament. He created canvas murals for the ceiling of the Opera in Paris, in addition to two large canvas murals for the lobby of the Metropolitan Opera House in New York City.

About the Media

Chagall usually worked in oils on canvas. He also created stained-glass windows, and designed costumes for ballet dancers.

About the Technique

Chagall often remembered things from his childhood and drew them on canvas. He covered whole canvases with many pictures of different sizes. He sometimes drew people with just one big eye or animals that looked like monsters. He painted them in bright colors, such as red, blue, and yellow.

John Steuart Curry
1897–1946

John Steuart Curry (jân stoō´ ərt kər´ ē) was born on a farm in Dunavant, Kansas, in 1897. Though he worked hard as a child, Curry was not very studious and instead liked to draw the animals and natural phenomena around him. He worked on a railroad to earn enough money to attend the Art Institute of Chicago and Geneva College. After his schooling he earned money as an illustrator for popular western magazine stories. He turned his attention to regionalism in the 1930s, capturing the everyday life and endurance of American heartlanders, especially during the Depression. Though he is best known for his regionalist paintings, Curry was also a painter of portraits and murals in both the East and the Midwest.

About Art History

Thomas Benton and Grant Wood were recognized as Curry's regionalist contemporaries. Many artists in the 1920s and 1930s were experimenting with abstraction, but these three men continued as realists and depicted their fellow Americans. Curry exhibited his work in Kansas, Connecticut, and New York, and was the first artist-in-residence at the School of Agriculture at the University of Wisconsin.

About the Artwork

Two of Curry's most famous paintings, *Baptism in Kansas* and *Tornado over Kansas,* were created from memory and were regarded as innovative in subject matter, but primitive in their hint of illustration. The focus Curry placed on the worker is evident in many of his paintings, although he also infused a sense of the spectacular into his series of circus paintings made after touring New England with the Ringling Brothers' Circus during the early 1930s.

About the Media

In addition to oils, Curry also worked in watercolors and pencil.

About the Technique

For his canvas paintings, Curry spent time observing his sources and making many sketches. Although he lived for some time in the city, he would often return to his parents' farm to observe and to generate ideas. Many of his paintings were created after he had sketched the scene much earlier, and a few of his paintings were created completely from memory. Curry planned his murals on paper and in sketches before drawing and painting them on walls.

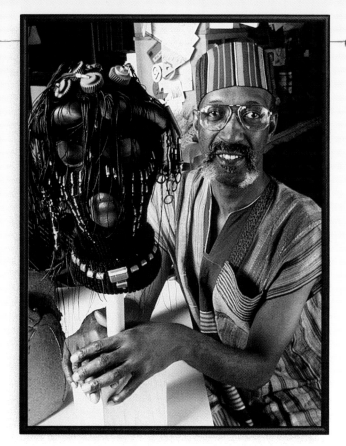

Willis "Bing" Davis
b. 1937

Bing Davis (bing dā´ vəs) was born in Dayton, Ohio. He was a student with many talents and gifts, including those for athletics and the arts. Because he excelled in sports, he was awarded a scholarship to DePauw University in Indiana, where he earned a degree in art education. He continued to study and earned his master's degree from Miami University in Oxford, Ohio. Davis has pioneered such projects as the Dayton-based, now nationwide, program Artists in the Schools. Davis has had more than 50 one-man exhibitions since 1959.

About Art History

Davis's style is a combination of African and African American styles. A fellowship to the country of Nigeria led him to explore the customs and heritage of his ancestors. This understanding of where he comes from spiritually and ethnically is incorporated into his artwork.

About the Artwork

Davis's artwork pays tribute to his African heritage. He transfers his ideas from one medium to the next. For example, he approaches much of his work in clay in the same way as he does collage, working with similar patterns and themes. Davis is more concerned with the messages in his art than with preparing works for exhibition.

About the Media

Davis works with a wide range of media. He is a ceramicist, photographer, jewelry maker, painter, and graphic artist. Drawing from an unlimited source of media allows Davis freedom of expression. He also relies a great deal on found objects to express the message of his artwork to the viewer.

About the Technique

Many of Davis's artistic works have come from an inquiry into his heritage. His art has been called "visual music." It is difficult to pinpoint one single technique for Davis. His methods are a reflection of the diversity he sees in the world. His ever-changing technique accommodates his ever-changing global perspective.

Edgar Degas
1834–1917

Edgar Degas (ed′ gär dā gä′) was born in Paris, France, to a wealthy family. He studied law for a short time before discovering his interest in painting. Degas studied briefly at the École des Beaux-Arts in Paris around 1855. He worked at an artist's studio and traveled widely to study art. His early work showed a concern with classical painting, in subject matter as well as composition. His themes always dealt with people and city life, especially dancers at the theater. After 1909, Degas turned to sculpture due to failing eyesight. He left many wax models of dancers and horses that were cast in bronze after his death.

▲ **Edgar Degas.** (French). *Self Portrait.*

Sterling and Francine Clark Art Institute, Williamstown, Massachusetts.

About Art History

Degas joined the impressionist group and exhibited with them, even though he detested the name and never painted in a purely impressionistic style. He admired Italian Renaissance painters, such as Leonardo da Vinci. He also admired the French neoclassical painter Ingres, whose figures had the grace of Greek statues. In his own work Degas combined impressionism with the painting style of the Renaissance.

About the Artwork

Degas is famous for his portraits, especially those of ballet dancers. Unlike other impressionists, he enjoyed painting genre scenes of modern life. His painting of customers in a hat shop, for example, was unusual. At that time artists did not usually paint such ordinary places.

About the Media

Degas created oil paintings, pastel drawings, ink drawings, and bronze sculptures. He also produced a great number of lithographs, engravings, and monotypes.

About the Technique

Many impressionists painted outdoors and quickly. Degas chose to work slowly in his studio. He planned his pictures and completed sketches before he painted. He sometimes took paintings back after they had been sold so he could improve them. He applied paint sketchily to make his work look unplanned.

Degas wanted his subjects to look as if they did not know they were being painted. He cut figures off at the edges of the canvas to make his composition seem spontaneous and not posed. He also wanted viewers to feel as if they were part of the picture. For this reason, Degas included large, open spaces to welcome viewers into his paintings.

Arthur Dove
1880–1946

Arthur Dove (är´ thər duv) was born and raised in upstate New York and received his first painting lessons from a neighbor. His father insisted that he study law in college, but Dove chose to pursue a career in art and was forced to support himself without help from his family. He moved to New York, where he worked as a freelance illustrator for popular magazines and later was introduced to other artists influenced by European modernists. A love of nature and innovative style characterize Arthur Dove's artistic career. He is regarded as the first abstract painter in America.

About Art History

In 1908, Dove traveled to Europe and was immediately inspired by the bright color and decorative patterning of Henri Matisse and the fauves. After returning to America in 1909, Dove joined a small group of progressive artists supported by Alfred Stieglitz and began creating abstract, nonobjective paintings which he first exhibited in 1912. Few people understood his early work, although Stieglitz and Georgia O'Keeffe continued to support him. In 1931, Dove became one of three main artists exhibited in Stieglitz's new gallery and critics became more receptive of his work. That same year he acquired a wealthy patron, Duncan Phillips, who commissioned much of his later work.

About the Artwork

Dove's abstract paintings were reflections of his love for nature and were often of landscapes or organic subjects. He used calligraphic line in his work to give a composition energy, and his colors tended to be bold and flat. Overlapped shapes without compositional depth or a sense of space were typical of Dove's paintings. He wanted his work to have energy and spirit and capture the essence of nature, and these criteria remained consistent throughout his career. Dove also tried to capture forces of nature such as wind and sound and wanted his work to be like music for the eyes. His 1943 piece *Sun* uses bright, radiating colors and undulating lines to exude a sense of warmth and energy.

About the Media

Dove painted in watercolors and oils. Later in his career he experimented with assemblage and used materials including aluminum, tin, copper, glass, wood, fabric, and found objects.

About the Technique

Dove made color studies before completing his final paintings. These studies are like rough drafts that allow the artist to practice with color, composition, and materials.

Raoul Dufy
1877–1953

Raoul Dufy (rä ool´ dū´ fā) was born in Le Havre, France, to an impoverished but happy family. He had an early interest in art and a passion for drawing. At the age of 15, he enrolled at the Le Havre School of Fine Arts, where he met Georges Braque, who was a pioneer of cubism, along with Picasso. Braque became a lifelong friend and major artistic influence. In 1900, Dufy received a grant to attend the École des Beaux-Arts in Paris. His interest in impressionism was directed toward fauvism under the influence of Matisse in 1905. He also worked as an illustrator, fabric designer, and decorator. *Time* magazine awarded him the moniker "Grandaddy of Modern Chic."

About Art History

Dufy and a friend from school, Othon Friesz, studied the works of Boudin together in the Le Havre museum and later worked with him at Falaise. Dufy went on to work with Albert Marquet at Sainte-Adresse and Braque at l'Estaque. He joined Leon Bonnat's studio in 1900, and in 1902 was introduced to Berthe Weill, who showed Dufy's work in her gallery.

About the Artwork

Dufy's favorite subjects included beach scenes, palm trees, race courses, and orchestras. His paintings of towns in the south of France are rendered with a charm that evidences his admiration.

About the Media

Dufy usually worked in oils on canvas.

About the Technique

Dufy expressed his fondness for pure color in his paintings. He developed a personal style, which produced rapid but precise drawings of frequently changing perspectives. He applied bright colors liberally and freely. These bright colors and fluid brushstrokes are hallmarks of his works.

Marisol Escobar

b. 1930

The Venezuelan family of Marisol Escobar (mar´ ǝ sōl ās kō bär´) often moved and led a life of comfort despite the economic hardships of the Depression. Escobar was born in Paris, France. When her mother died in 1941, her family moved first to Venezuela and then to California, where she attended a girls' school. It was there that she began to infuse religion into her study of art. Escobar was encouraged by her father to study art, and she attended the École des Beaux-Arts in Paris before deciding to move to New York City, with its vibrant arts culture, in 1950. Her painting and drawing gave way to sculpting and creating installations. Escobar continues to create art with a wide range of materials in New York.

About Art History

When she studied in New York, Escobar's mentor was Hans Hofmann, and she was well acquainted with many leading abstract expressionists, especially Willem de Kooning. Pre-colombian artifacts inspired her experiment with found objects, terra-cotta clay, and plaster casting. In an era dominated by abstract expressionist painters, Escobar established her own identity by instilling humor in her three-dimensional art. In the 1960s, she joined the company of pop artists Roy Lichtenstein and Andy Warhol, although she avoided using commercial items in her own work.

About the Artwork

Escobar's sculptures in the 1960s and 1970s were often of her family, friends, world leaders, and famous artists, as shown in her piece *The Family*. Although often humorous, her art at times focuses on the harsh reality experienced by disadvantaged or minority groups, such as Dust Bowl immigrants, poor Cuban families, and Native Americans. Escobar has also designed stage sets for plays.

About the Media

Escobar taught herself how to use terra-cotta clay and how to work with wood, which is utilized in a number of her sculptures. Her wooden figures are often painted and connected with found objects, which range widely from articles of clothing to umbrellas. She also uses natural materials, such as stone, plaster, charcoal, and cloth.

About the Technique

For her wooden sculptures Escobar uses woodcutting tools to shape the bodies of her subjects, and then applies oil paints to their faces. Sometimes she uses smooth, polished wood or papier-mâché for parts of her figures. For her portraits, Escobar studies and sketches her subjects in pencil or charcoal before adding color.

Lavinia Fontana
1552–1614

Lavinia Fontana (lə vin´ ē ə fon´ tä nə) was one of the first women to have a successful career as an artist. She was able to support herself and her family by painting. She received major commissions from public and private patrons for portraits and religious subjects. Fontana studied art with her father, Prospero Fontana, an artist and teacher. It was in her father's studio that she met another student, Gian Paolo Zappi, whom she married in 1577. Zappi gave up his artistic career to assist his wife in her studio. He handled the accounts of her many commissions and helped care for their 11 children. At the height of her career in 1603, Fontana and her family moved to Rome at the invitation of Pope Clement VIII.

▲ **Lavinia Fontana** (Italian).
Self Portrait of the Artist. c. 1595.

Oil on canvas. Galleria degli Uffiz, Florence, Italy.

About Art History

Most Renaissance art is visually realistic. Using *chiaroscuro* (a range of color tones from highlights to shadows) artists created the illusion that the figures they painted were actually three-dimensional. Portraits of women were often betrothal or marriage portraits. The lavishness of a woman's dress and jewelry would indicate the wealth and status of her father or husband.

About the Artwork

Portrait of a Noblewoman, painted around 1580, is characteristic of Fontana's many depictions of women. The unidentified young woman stands with her gaze modestly turned away from the viewer. One hand caresses a small lap dog and the other holds a marten skin adorned with an exquisitely jeweled head. A marten is an arboreal animal that is a relative of the weasel. Marten skins were a popular fashion accessory of the time and can often be seen in Renaissance portraits of upper-class women.

About the Media

Fontana worked in oil on canvas. By the sixteenth century in Italy, oil paint on canvas had replaced the tempera paint on wooden panels that was typical of earlier centuries.

About the Technique

Fontana skillfully depicted contrasting textures in her work. She carefully rendered each detail, and in many of her portraits the background is uniformly dark and flat.

Viola Frey
b. 1933

Viola Frey (vī ō´ lə frī) was born in Lodi, California, on a farm and vineyard. She grew up with strong female role models and became a collector of found objects. She especially likes collecting little figurines from flea markets, and she inserts these objects into ceramic assemblage artwork. These sculptures represent the way the modern world has come to depend on material goods. Frey's large ceramic human figures also reference or critique the modern world and are often covered with symbols and textures that give them an appearance similar to assemblage.

About Art History

Frey studied painting with Richard Diebenkorn at the California College of Arts and Crafts, then focused on ceramics at Tulane University, where she studied with Katherine Choy. In 1958, she went with Choy to the New York Clay Art Center, where she pursued her studies in sculpture, but realized that the center for the ceramic movement was on the west coast. She moved back to California and became interested in the figurative movement practiced by artists such as Diebenkorn and Joan Brown. In the 1980s Frey began making her famous monumental human sculptures that now reside in public and private collections around the world.

About the Artwork

Frey is predominantly a sculptor and enjoys creating works that represent the human figure. Grandmothers, spirals, figurines, horses, businessmen, monsters, the mind, the world, age, beauty, and ugliness are just some of the subjects and themes of her work. She often sculpts monumental figures of women or men in business suits, creating them in such a large scale that they seem to tower over viewers like adults peering down at children. To Frey, her larger-than-life women represent the self-determination and authority of all women and serve as an avenue of social critique. The energetic brushwork and brightly colored symbols adorning her figurative sculptures further emphasize their strength, as seen in her ceramic piece *Family Portrait.*

About the Media

Both Frey's large and small sculptures are ceramic creations. Some are hand-built, and others are slip-cast. Frey also makes drawings, assemblages, and decorative, biographical ceramic plates.

About the Technique

It takes Frey about a year to complete a monumental figurative sculpture. She paints energetic symbols with energetic colors. For her assemblages, Frey accumulates lots of found objects over time and assembles them into a sculpture or work of art, relying on the combined meaning of all the objects to give the final piece its identity.

Elizabeth Garrison
b. 1914

Elizabeth Garrison (i li´ zə beth ga´ re sən) earned a teaching certificate from a two-year college in 1932, and began teaching in the small town of Benevolence, Georgia. She was paid $50 a month for eight months of work in a small country school where she taught Grades 1 through 4 in one room. Out of that $50, she paid $15 room and board, saved money to go to summer school, and helped to pay a younger brother's tuition in an Alabama prep school. After two years of teaching, she received a scholarship to go to school full time to finish her four-year degree.

◄ **Elizabeth Garrison.** (American). *Georgia.* 1983.

Cotton. $4 \times 5\frac{1}{4}$ feet (1.22 × 1.6 m.).
St. Simons Island Historical Museum of Georgia,
St. Simons Island, Georgia.

About Art History

As a classroom teacher, Garrison taught elementary and high school classes. She taught school and raised her family wherever her husband's career led them. She loved teaching science because her students were fascinated by the subject. After earning her doctoral degree, she finished her teaching career as a professor of elementary education in the School of Education at Georgia Southern University. She had always sewn and done handwork, such as embroidery and crocheting. She had never quilted, however, until she visited a quilt store in 1975 and could not afford to buy the quilt she wanted—so she set out to make it herself. Not many instruction books were available in 1975 that we have today, so she had to learn by trial and error—and she felt that she made a lot of errors. Today there are many resources to learn quilting.

About the Artwork

Garrison's *Georgia* quilt was designed for the two-hundred and fiftieth birthday of the state of Georgia quilting competition. She had been taking her science students to visit the Skidaway Island Marine Education Center for several years, and had collected interesting materials. Her quilt won first place in its field. The St. Simons Island Historical Museum of Georgia purchased it, and it is still displayed there today.

About the Technique

When the quilting competition was announced, Garrison choose the coastal area as her category for the competition. She was about to leave on a freighter trip to South America, but she made her sketches, selected her fabrics, and took all her work on the trip. While on board, she assembled all the small pieces and embroidered the details on them. When she returned to Georgia she sewed the fabrics together and did all the hand stitching. She completed the quilt just in time for the competition.

Paul Gauguin
1848–1903

As one of France's leading postimpressionist painters, the artistic career of Paul Gauguin (pôl gō gan´) did not begin until he was a 25-year-old stockbroker. He decided to become a painter when he saw the first impressionist exhibit in Paris, France, in 1874, and throughout the next 30 years he developed his own style independent from impressionism and full of influences and experiences from his life. He was not content or fulfilled in Europe, however, and in 1891 he left his family and job to move to Tahiti and various other destinations in the South Pacific. With the exception of a two-year absence, Gauguin remained in Tahiti for the rest of his life, painting until his death in 1903.

About Art History

Through his encounters and friendship with van Gogh, Pissarro, and Cézanne, Gauguin developed a passion for expression through color. In the 1880s, he painted in France and created landscapes similar to those of Pissarro.

About the Artwork

Gauguin's style is a conceptual method of representation. His subjects, mainly women, are painted in flat, bold colors emphasizing a wild, almost untamed environment. His exposure to primitive art in Tahiti can clearly be seen in the rich colors in pieces such as *Faaturuma.* A woman's surroundings are painted in bright, earthy tones and her dress is a warm rose color that brings her image even closer to the viewer. Gauguin's ties with impressionism were, at this point, behind him. He had finally found his own style in a new land.

About the Media

Gauguin's portraits were created in oils on canvas. When he painted in France, he also used pastels for some of his landscapes.

About the Technique

The colorful, flat appearance of Gauguin's paintings was achieved by using large brushes and brushstrokes. Many of his paintings were created by sketching and studying models, and the expressive nature of his surfaces reflects the influence of the primitive art of the South Pacific.

Domenico Ghirlandaio

1449–1494

Domenico Ghirlandaio (dō mā´ nē kō gēr län´ dä ō) was born in Florence, Italy, in 1449. He was the son of Tommaso Bigordi, a goldsmith. *Ghirlandaio* means "garland maker." This name was given to Tommaso because of his expertise in designing silver wreaths for women to wear in their hair. Domenico inherited his father's nickname, Ghirlandaio. He developed his technique in painting and in mosaic while studying with Alesso Baldovinetti, a distinguished painter in Florence. Ghirlandaio lived in Florence most of his life, achieving great success as an artist.

▲ **Domenico Ghirlandaio.** (Italian).
Detail, *Adoration of the Shepherds.* 1485.

Tempera on panel. Sassetti Chapel, Santa Trinita, Florence, Italy.

About Art History

Ghirlandaio was not one to experiment. He learned from past artists and used their techniques in his work. He painted in a direct and detailed style. His style was less complex than that of other major Florentine artists of his time, such as Botticelli.

About the Artwork

Like other Renaissance painters Ghirlandaio is best known for his religious paintings. He painted such subjects as the Virgin Mary and The Last Supper. When painting faces, he used three-quarter and full-face poses. In a three-quarter pose the face is slightly turned.

About the Media

Ghirlandaio painted on prepared wooden panels. He used oil and tempera paints, which he made by hand. He also created fresco murals.

About the Technique

Ghirlandaio first created an outline of his subject, then filled in the lines with paint.

Duane Hanson
1925–1996

Duane Hanson (dwān han´ sən) carved little figures out of logs using kitchen knives as a boy in his native Minnesota. Later he attended art school and taught art in Atlanta, Georgia and Miami, Florida. The same art dealer who discovered Andy Warhol arranged for Hanson's first solo exhibition. His life-size sculptures of ordinary people were an immediate success with the public. People could identify with his work. Hanson married and had five children. He continued to plan and create sculpture until the end of his life.

About Art History

Hanson's super-realistic style is so successful that people try to start conversations with his sculptures. One time a museum visitor dialed 911 to get help for an "unconscious" Hanson sculpture.

About the Artwork

Hanson created more than 100 sculptures during his career. His subjects were real people, ranging from janitors to sunbathers to athletes. One example is *Tourists,* a life-size and lifelike man and woman dressed in clashing clothing. Hanson's aim was to make viewers more aware of themselves and others. In a lighthearted way he tried to warn viewers not to want so much that they can never be happy.

About the Media

Hanson used a combination of polyester resin and fiberglass to create his sculptures.

About the Technique

Hanson often took six weeks or more to construct a sculpture. He began by choosing a model, often one of his friends. He posed the person and covered the model's body with petroleum jelly to keep the mold from sticking to the skin. He formed the mold by applying plaster bandages to parts of the model until he had made a mold of the model's whole body. After each mold dried and hardened, he removed it. Then he filled the plaster mold with a flesh-colored mixture of polyester resin and fiberglass to form the sculpture. After reassembling the parts, he painted the figure. Finally he added glass eyes, clothing, a wig, and accessories.

Childe Hassam
1859–1935

Childe Hassam (chīld has´ əm) was born in Dorchester, Massachusetts. During high school he began work as an accountant. When his father's hardware store burned down he needed to make more money, so he became a wood engraver's apprentice. His natural artistic talent helped him become a freelance illustrator while studying drawing and painting with William Rimmer and Ignaz Gaugengigl. Hassam painted in Paris, France, for a few years, and upon his return to America, he settled in New York City. In 1889 he joined a group of impressionists called the Ten American Painters, who exhibited together each year for 20 years. Hassam won many prizes and awards for his work and was elected associate of the National Academy of Design in 1902.

About Art History

When Hassam studied with Gaugengigl, a Bavarian painter, he was influenced by the new realism that was being taught to many Americans abroad. Followers of this movement sought to return to the techniques of the Dutch and Spanish masters. His time abroad exposed him to the work of the French impressionists—painters who created candid paintings showing sunlight's effect on natural settings. Hassam went on to become the most famous impressionist painter in New York City.

About the Artwork

Hassam's most famous paintings were created near the beginning of the twentieth century. He painted New York City's streets, parades, neighborhoods, and skyline. Unlike the French impressionists, who focused on sunny scenes, he often painted drizzly city evenings.

About the Media

Hassam's artwork during the 1870s and 1880s included mostly drawings and watercolors, but he later worked with oils. He also created prints, etchings, engravings, and lithographs.

About the Technique

Like most impressionists, Hassam used a light palette of colors and broken strokes to create his paintings. Impressionists sought to show an image of an instant as seen by the sensitive eye of the artist.

Robert Henri
1865–1929

Robert Henri (rob´ ərt hen´ rē) was born Robert Henry Cozad in Cincinnati, Ohio. He changed his name when his father was accused of murder. Henri showed great artistic talent at a young age and was encouraged by his parents to pursue painting at the Pennsylvania Academy of Fine Arts, and later the Academie Julian and École des Beaux-Arts in Paris, France. When he returned from Paris, he became a widely known and respected teacher, emphasizing the importance of his students' creative freedom. He also stressed his own artistic freedom and founded The Eight, a group of American artists who joined his rebellion against the strict confines of academic art.

About Art History

Henri began his artistic career under the influence of his teacher, Thomas Anshutz, who believed American art should be independent of European domination. After his return from Paris in 1902, Henri taught at the Chase School of Art, the New York School of Art, and the Women's School of Design, where he began his fight against academic art. In 1909, he formed his own art school called *The Eight,* a group comprised of artists who believed art should be relevant to contemporary life. These artists came to be known as the *Ashcan School* and included Arthur B. Davies, William Glackens, Ernest Lawson, George Luks, Maurice Prendergast, Everett Shinn, and John Sloan. As a teacher and an artist Henri believed that people with real talent should be given the opportunity to exhibit, and he worked toward this goal throughout his life.

About the Artwork

The Ashcan School believed that art should apply to everyday life and reflect its reality, not just the popular tastes of the National Academy of Design.

Henri's art embodies this sentiment. He was influenced by the Dutch painter Franz Hals and painted in a realistic manner called *social realism.* His paintings were primarily urban portraits and genre pieces, depicting people's personalities with vitality and spontaneous honesty, as seen in his portrait, *Bernadita.* As a change from painting portraits, Henri sometimes created landscapes, although his true passion was depicting human beings as they really were.

About the Media

Henri's depictions of urban life were created in oils on canvas and his landscapes were created in pastels.

About the Technique

In his classes Henri would promote tonal styles rather than colorist styles, and he painted quickly by slashing thick paint onto his canvas to capture the strength of the moment.

Winslow Homer
1835–1910

Winslow Homer (winz´ lō hō´ mər) was born in Boston. He had very little formal training in art, but he showed great artistic talent even in his earliest sketches. He worked as a magazine illustrator for nearly 20 years. When the Civil War began, *Harper's Weekly* sent him to the front lines to sketch both the fighting and ordinary life. Homer did not begin to paint seriously until he was 26. He taught himself the techniques he needed, and eventually settled on the Maine coast. In his later years Homer lived like a hermit, seldom seeing anyone.

About Art History

Homer avoided other artists, other art styles, and art exhibitions. He once said, "If one wishes to become a real artist, one must never look at the work of another artist." His first paintings were very detailed. His later work was simpler and more creative. Homer led American art out of the romanticism of the mid-1800s and into the peak of realism.

About the Artwork

Homer loved nature, especially the sea. Even though he lived in New York City, he never painted city scenes. Instead he painted scenes from nature. Over the years he changed from painting families in farm scenes to painting people struggling with nature, usually the sea. During this period he painted *The Fog Warning*, which shows a man alone in a small boat on a rough sea. Toward the end of his life, Homer stopped putting people in his paintings. Instead, he focused only on nature.

About the Media

Homer is best known for his watercolors, but he also created sketches, wood engravings, and oil paintings. He also worked in charcoal, chalk, and pencil.

About the Technique

Homer was very patient and particular about details. He waited for months for the light to be just right when he was painting *Early Morning at Sea*. He used watercolors in an unusual way for his time. Instead of filling in light areas with white paint, he left the paper white.

Jasper Johns
b. 1930

Jasper Johns (jas´ pər jänz) was born in Augusta, Georgia. After serving in Japan with the United States Army, he moved to New York City. There he worked in a bookstore and started creating art. When he was 24, he decided to throw away all the art he had ever made. He wanted a fresh start. He was determined to create original art, not copies of the styles of other artists. Since then Johns has been known for his inventiveness.

About Art History

Johns is one of the most important artists in the American pop art movement. Pop artists use everyday objects as the subjects of art. They reject abstract painting styles and techniques like splattering paint on canvases. Pop artists focus on American mass culture, including television, billboard advertising, and cars.

About the Artwork

Much of Johns's artwork shows familiar items such as books, flags, targets, numbers, and maps. He gives an object new meaning by challenging the viewer to look at and study the object rather than use it.

About the Media

Johns varies his media from work to work. In some works he uses a palette knife to apply wax mixed with paint onto the canvas. In other works he uses oil paints. Johns has sculptures cast in bronze.

About the Technique

Early in his career, Johns used precise lines and built up paint in thick layers on his canvases. His later paintings are less exact and more abstract. Johns has also made realistic bronze sculptures of commonplace objects such as coffee cans.

Ben Jones

b. 1942

Ben Jones (ben jōnz) was born in Paterson, New Jersey. He showed his potential as an artist as early as the age of five. His early career plan was to become an interpreter of French and Spanish. In high school he was encouraged by his art teacher, Rosalind Feinstein, to pursue a career in the arts. After college, Jones went on to participate in many group and solo exhibitions. He has traveled back and forth to Africa many times. African culture and Jones's African American heritage are strong parts of his artistic identity.

About Art History

Jones is a postmodern artist. His work does not follow any set rules or structures. In the spirit of Marcel Duchamp, Jones believes that found objects are an important part of art. He thinks the idea of what art is should always be changing and expanding.

About the Artwork

Jones believes whatever idea he has in mind will affect the decision of what material he will use to construct the piece. Themes that run through his work are Africa, his spirituality, political ideas, and thoughts about the tension of two- and three-dimensional space. Although he is highly influenced by African motifs, Jones does not try to imitate them. His work focuses on spiritual healing, self-renewal, and faith.

About the Media

Jones works in mixed media, including acrylics, watercolors, found objects, collage, and plaster.

About the Technique

Jones's technique, like his ideas, is always changing. He combines many different textures and objects. His creative freedom is unlimited because he works with so many different media.

Frida Kahlo
1907–1954

Frida Kahlo (frē´ dä kā´ lō) was born in Mexico. Her life was short and painful. As a child she had polio, which caused one leg to stop growing. At 18, she was severely injured in a bus accident. Thirty-two operations did not ease her pain entirely and it often kept her in bed. Whenever possible she dressed in richly embroidered outfits, wore much jewelry, and tucked flowers in her hair. At 22, she married the famous painter Diego Rivera. He was 42 at the time and had been married twice before. Kahlo and Rivera lived in separate houses connected by a bridge. Despite their stormy relationship, she wanted to have children and was deeply disappointed that they could not. After winning wide recognition for her painting, the frail Kahlo died at age 47.

About Art History

Kahlo is often grouped with the surrealists, but she was more interested in personal expression than dreams and fantasies. She used symbols to represent her feelings. For example, a skeleton, representing death, often appeared in her work. She also created an imaginary friend, her twin. She showed the twins sitting together in the painting *The Two Fridas.* An artery joins their exposed hearts.

About the Artwork

Kahlo used her life as the subject for much of her work. She painted her own birth, her bus accident, her marriage to Rivera, and scenes depicting her physical pain. Kahlo said she painted portraits of herself because she was often alone.

About the Media

Kahlo worked in oils on small canvases, often about the size of a sheet of paper.

About the Technique

Kahlo painted precisely, carefully controlling her brushstrokes. In her later work she used specific colors to express emotional states. Yellow expressed madness, sickness, and fear. Cobalt blue represented love.

Elizabeth Paulos-Krasle

b. 1964

Elizabeth Paulos-Krasle (i li´ zə bəth kraz´ əl) was born in 1964 in British Columbia, Canada. She was raised on a fruit orchard in Spences Bridge, British Columbia. She would often pass the time making clay sculptures and bowls from the soil. Her mother taught her how to sew, knit, and crochet in the Portuguese tradition, visually copying a pattern rather than reading it. Clay was one of Paulos-Krasle's favorite mediums in high school and college. While studying at the University of Victoria and the University of Georgia, she enjoyed hand building pieces from clay. Today she teaches art at the primary level, and continues to develop her artwork through many different media.

About Art History

During the twentieth century, artists began experimenting with every imaginable combination of subject matter and materials as they extended and challenged the boundaries of traditional art forms. Artists redefined sculpture as they created original works of art inspired by pop culture and their own imaginations. The increased movement toward freedom of expression throughout the decades of the 1960s, 70s, and 80s has allowed and encouraged sculptors to create works with unlimited possibilities.

About the Artwork

Puff is a ceramic bank. The subject matter of the dragon and the cartoonish style of the piece are whimsical in nature.

About the Media

The ceramic sculpture *Puff* is made of clay, paint, and a ceramic glaze.

About the Technique

Paulos-Krasle often uses textures from nature to imprint patterns onto clay, and hand builds each sculpture.

Le Corbusier
1887-1965

Le Corbusier (lə kor bōōs yā´) is a pseudonym for Charles Edouard Jeanneret (shärl ādwär zhan nə rā). He was born in La Chaux-de-Fonds, Switzerland, and took the name *Corbusier* from a relative. A teacher encouraged him to study architecture. Le Corbusier traveled around Europe to study classical architecture on his teacher's advice. Between 1908 and 1909 he studied architecture in Paris. In 1910 he studied in Berlin, Germany. After World War I he settled in Paris. He became a French citizen in 1930. From 1921 to 1945, Le Corbusier and his cousin ran an architecture workshop. Architects from all over the world came to talk to him.

About Art History

Le Corbusier was an important modern architect known around the world. He designed functional yet monumental buildings. These buildings were based on geometric principles and mathematical proportions. He liked the idea of high-rises and large buildings surrounded by city parks. Le Corbusier was also a painter and author. He wrote for *L'Esprit,* a French magazine of contemporary thought, between 1920 and 1925. Later he expanded the articles into books on architecture, painting, and urban planning.

About the Artwork

Le Corbusier was one of the first to relate a building's architectural design to its function. This included experimenting with building materials. From his early studies in Paris, Le Corbusier learned about working with reinforced concrete. Toward the middle of his professional career, Le Corbusier became more interested in geometric principles using cubist forms of glass and stucco to enclose a reinforced concrete frame. His interest in geometric rules carried through to his late career, but his interest in monumental design was simplified to a rougher concrete exterior.

About the Technique

Early in his career Le Corbusier used tracing paper to determine the proportional relationship of windows and doors to the outside of a building. Le Corbusier created screen walls independent of the building's structural frame. He experimented with ceiling heights, and put colored panels inside and outside buildings.

Mitch Lyons

With an extensive background in ceramics, Mitch Lyons (mich līˊ ənz) established his own studio and gallery and produced handmade pots from 1971 to 1976. After experimenting with clay and printmaking in 1975, he shifted his focus to his new clay monoprint technique. As a colorist, Lyons creates prints that showcase saturated fields of layered color and builds each new composition upon the foundation of earlier prints. For the last twenty years, Lyons has been creating his innovative clay prints from his studio in Pennsylvania.

About Art History

Lyons earned an undergraduate degree in printmaking and a master's of fine arts degree in ceramics. His interest in both of these media eventually led to the development of a new clay print technique. In 1980 he built a leather-hard clay slab that provides the basis for each of his prints and retains the impressions of old pieces in each new clay print he rolls. When he began this technique, his working slab was a quarter-inch thick. It is now more than two inches thick.

About the Artwork

Lyons' monoprints are saturated with color and markmaking and can be identified by their gestural layers of color. Lyons primarily creates nonobjective works, or compositions without recognizable subject matter, though a few of his pieces contain representational or realistic subjects. His compositions are not consciously planned, as most prints are, for Lyons relies on the role of chance in his work. Most of his clay prints, such as *Slip Trail,* feature asymmetrical balance and an emphasis on fields of color.

About the Media

Lyons creates his prints on a large kaolin clay slab that reaches dimensions of fifty-four square feet. Instead of glazing his work, he uses pigment-permeated clay to generate his own new colors and clay pastels. He mixes slip, or liquid clay, with inorganic pigments to attain his desired colors and then rolls it into a slab to form the composition for his print.

About the Technique

Lyons uses the same large, leather-hard clay tablet as a table and building block for each of his clay prints. With everyday materials, simple tools, and handmade stencils, Lyons creates progressive prints. He sometimes sifts pastels over a stencil to achieve even more layering and texture in a piece. After his composition of clay is made, he rolls the clay out flat and lays a wet *ground* (a synthetic interfacing material) over the design. He then vigorously rubs the ground into the design, which transfers the print from the slab to the two-dimensional material. Thicker clay will often adhere to the flat material and remain as a textural element in the final print.

Manabu Mabe
1924–1997

Manabu Mabe (mä nä bōō mä´ be) was born in Kumamoto, Japan. In 1934, he moved with his family to Brazil. In São Paulo, Mabe worked on a coffee plantation. He painted landscapes and still lifes in his free time. In the late 1950s, he won recognition from critics for his abstract paintings. He had many solo shows in art galleries and was featured in exhibitions worldwide.

About Art History

São Paulo, Brazil, has the largest Japanese population of any city outside Japan. It is the center of an art movement based on the Eastern traditions of calligraphy and appreciation of surface textures. A group called SEIBI (São Paulo Association of Japanese Artists) had its first show in 1938. Members of SEIBI included Mabe, Tomie Ohtake, and Kazuo Wakabayashi, among other artists born in Japan.

About the Artwork

In his earliest paintings Mabe created realistic landscapes and still lifes. Later he began to focus on more abstract art. Mabe combined symbols and colors from Japan and Brazil to create unique images. He used bright, vibrant colors that reminded viewers of the tropical plants of Brazil.

He added symbolism to his work by including marks that resemble Japanese calligraphy. He filled his canvases with large planes of color set at unusual diagonal angles.

About the Media

Mabe worked in oils and acrylics on canvas.

About the Technique

Mabe painted abstract, colorful paintings on large canvases. He created strong contrasts of light and shadow. Then he added splashes of white, graphic marks, and blobs and drips of color. Mabe used many layers of paint, and his brushstrokes can be seen on the surfaces of his canvases.

Robert McCall
b. 1919

Robert McCall (ro´ bərt mə kôl´) was born in Columbus, Ohio. He studied art at The Columbus Art School for two years. He is interested in the wonder of the universe and the mysteries of space. Along with other artists, McCall was invited by NASA to observe the development of the space program. His drawings and paintings recorded the wonder and excitement everyone felt about exploring space. As one of the official artists of the U.S. space program, he has painted pictures of space travel for more than 30 years. He has also designed postage stamps for the U.S. government. He recently designed a large wall of stained-glass windows with his wife, Louise, who is also an artist.

About Art History

McCall is a graphic artist and painter. He creates pictures for companies, magazines, movies, and museums. He has produced paintings for movies, including *Star Trek* and *2001: A Space Odyssey.* Many of McCall's space paintings are murals— very large pictures painted directly on walls. Many tourists have seen his murals at the Smithsonian Institution's National Air and Space Museum in Washington, D.C., and at EPCOT Center in Orlando, Florida.

About the Artwork

McCall has drawn many pictures of launching rockets. He also completed many paintings of astronauts inside spaceships. Because he includes a great deal of detail in his work, his paintings look very realistic.

About the Media

McCall makes many drawings to prepare for his paintings. He paints with oils and acrylics on canvas, and also paints murals. He has done work in stained glass, watercolors, and ink.

About the Technique

McCall watches spaceships take off from Cape Canaveral and then draws his impressions of the events. He uses many crisp, bright colors, such as blues and oranges, to make the explosions look powerful and hot. For pictures inside the spacecraft, he draws every wrinkle in every spacesuit and every knob on every control panel. He paints slowly and carefully.

Irene Preston Miller and the Hudson River Quilters

Irene Preston Miller (ī´ rēn pres´ tən mi´ lər), an avid quilter and seamstress, was involved with the publication of a number of sewing and quilting instruction books. One of her most substantial and well-known pieces is the *Hudson River Quilt*, which she and a group of 30 women, the Hudson River Quilters, created together.

◀ **Irene Preston Miller and the Hudson River Quilters.** (American). *The Hudson River Quilt.* 1969–1972.

Cotton, wool, and blends with cotton embroidery. $95\frac{1}{4} \times 80$ inches (241.95 × 203.2 cm.). American Folk Art Museum, New York, New York.

About Art History

Miller's *Hudson River Quilt* began its exhibition tour to museums and galleries around the world at the American Folk Art Museum in 1972. Its journeys and exhibitions helped raise funds and awareness for the Hudson River and surrounding landscape. In 1990, the Hudson River Quilters decided to sell the quilt at an auction to benefit three educational organizations in the Hudson River region. The people who bought it donated the quilt to the American Folk Art Museum, which suited its initial purpose because the museum is a public institution in the Hudson River Valley.

About the Artwork

The quilt was made between 1969 and 1972, and is similar to signature quilts sewn in the 1800s. Unlike the majority of nineteenth-century geometric and floral quilts, the *Hudson River Quilt* is entirely pictorial, like many of the quilts made since the 1960s. Miller's quilt is composed of individual, stitched fabric squares brought together by a blue sash that represents the river. The quilt blocks tell the story of the river's journey, beginning at its source in the Adirondack Mountains and ending in the New York City harbor.

About the Media

Cotton and wool thread and cotton fabric were used to make the *Hudson River Quilt.*

About the Technique

Initially the women who formed the Hudson River Quilters were chosen more for their interest in preserving the Hudson River than their sewing skills. Their skills grew as they created fabric squares, or *blocks,* for the quilt. The Hudson River Quilters stitched each square by hand and then fit them together to form the quilt in a process called *piecing.*

Joan Miró
1893–1983

Joan Miró (hō´ än mē rō´) entered art school in his native Spain when he was a teenager. His teachers introduced him to modern art, but in time he developed his own style, moving from traditional painting to surreal fantasy. Miró lived in Spain and France and focused entirely on his art. By the end of World War II he was very famous. He painted a wall-sized mural for Harvard University, and created two ceramic walls for the UNESCO building in Paris, France. Both the cities of Houston, Texas, and Chicago, Illinois, asked him to create huge sculptures. Miró received numerous awards for his artwork. He lived a quiet life, and although his work received much attention, Miró remained in the background. Creating art was his whole life.

About Art History

Miró was fascinated with symbols. He wanted to show nature as it would be painted by a primitive artist or a child. He was influenced by the dadaists, the surrealists, and Paul Klee's childlike drawings. Miró also encouraged many young artists— especially in the United States—to experiment and move away from realism.

About the Artwork

Miró began by painting landscapes, portraits, and still lifes. Later he moved on to create "dream pictures" and imaginary landscapes. In these, Miró showed his view of harsh modern life. Some of the shapes he painted look like amoeba or graffiti. Miró's work became simpler as he grew older. For example, one of his later paintings, *Blue II,* consists of several dots and an orange line on a blue surface.

About the Media

Miró expressed his fantasies through a wide variety of media. He created drawings, paintings, collages, lithographs, murals, tapestries, sculptures, and ceramic pieces. He even designed costumes and settings for the play *Romeo and Juliet.*

Amedeo Modigliani
1884–1920

Amedeo Modigliani (ä mä dä′ ō mô dēl yä′ nē) was born in Italy. He studied art in Italy and France. He eventually settled in Montmartre, a district in Paris, France where many artists lived. Modigliani began his art career as a painter but found that he enjoyed sculpting more. In 1915, he returned to painting. He sometimes reproduced his sculptures as paintings. Initially his artwork was not appreciated. He did not sell any paintings at his first and only exhibition, but he continued to paint in the same way until his death at age 35. Modigliani died of tuberculosis, but his health was already poor due to an excessive intake of alcohol and drugs. Now Modigliani's work is sought by art collectors who gladly pay high prices for single paintings.

About Art History

Modigliani was influenced by African art and by the work of Cézanne, Toulouse-Lautrec, and Picasso. His early work seemed to copy the style of his favorite artists. By 1909, however, he had developed his own style, which became more abstract as he got older.

About the Artwork

Modigliani focused on the human face in his paintings and sculptures. Of his 25 existing stone sculptures, 23 are sculptures of heads. His portraits are considered some of the finest art of the early 1900s. The subjects of his portraits included artists Diego Rivera and Pablo Picasso.

About the Media

Modigliani worked in oils and pencil and sculpted in wood and stone.

About the Technique

In his paintings and sculptures Modigliani often simplified his subjects' features and elongated their necks. He often left the eyes blank or filled them with criss-crossed lines. He expressed his subjects' personalities through their other facial features. By the end of his career Modigliani could create a portrait very swiftly by drawing only a dozen or so lines.

Berthe Morisot

1841–1865

Berthe Morisot (bârt môr ē´s ō) was born in France. She was the granddaughter of the painter Fragonard. Taught by her father, she learned how to draw when she was very young. Later she took painting lessons with her sister. She began selling her paintings when she was 23, but she never felt that she was treated as an equal of male painters. When she was 33, she married Eugene Manet, the brother of Édouard Manet. They had one daughter, Julie.

About Art History

Morisot was a pupil of the French realist painter Corot, but she was influenced primarily by Édouard Manet. She regularly exhibited with the impressionists, against the advice of her family and friends. These painters were interested in how light looked when it reflected off of objects. They often painted landscapes in light pastel colors like yellow, blue, and green. Morisot was friends with many artists, including Degas, who painted in the impressionist style. Morisot and Cassat are often considered the most important female painters of the nineteenth century. Édouard Manet was convinced by Morisot to change his palette and to abandon black.

About the Artwork

Morisot painted genre paintings of women in their homes wearing expensive dresses and hats. She also liked to paint images of people in gardens of trees, flowers, and bushes. She took advantage of how light played off these surfaces.

About the Media

Morisot generally painted in oil on canvas. She also made some paintings with watercolors, pastels, and hard steel pencils on paper.

About the Technique

Morisot made her paintings seem light and soft by working quickly. Her work looks like it is done with swift, sketchy strokes. Few contours or details were used. When she painted, she put a lot of paint on her brush, but she hardly touched the canvas. Sometimes she drew a scene in pencil first, and then painted patches of bright colors across the surface.

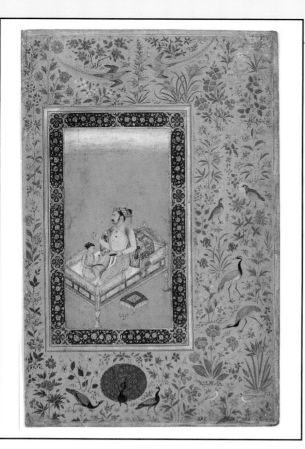

Nanha the Mughal

c. 1582–1635

Nanha the Mughal (nān´ hā the mū´ gəl) was an Indian artist who was skilled enough to remain a court painter during the reigns of three emperors—Akbar, Jahangir, and Shah Jahan. Nanha's nephew, Bishan Das, also became a portrait painter.

◀ **Nanha the Mughal.** (Indian). *Emperor Shah Jahan and His Son, Suja.* 1625–30.

Colors on gilt and paper. $15\frac{5}{16} \times 10\frac{5}{16}$ inches (38.89 × 26.19 cm.). The Metropolitan Museum of Art, New York, New York.

About Art History

Nanha's work is an excellent example of the Mughal, or Mogul, painting that was popular in India from the sixteenth to nineteenth centuries. Used mostly for book illustrations and miniature portraits, painters portrayed historic events, scenes from Persian and Indian literature and folktales, scenes of everyday life, and studies of natural life. Mughal painting showed the influence of Persian art but was more realistic and detailed. Mughal artists also studied the Western engravings and illustrated manuscripts brought to India by missionaries. In turn, Western painters, including Rembrandt, studied Mughal painting.

About the Artwork

Nanha was best known for his miniature portraits of royalty and nobles. He favored two figure types in his paintings—stocky and thickset, and slender with an expressive face. He also specialized in scenes showing lion attacks, such as *Perils of the Hunt.*

About the Media

Mughal painters used pigments made from minerals and vegetables mixed with a gummy substance. They made brushes from the tail hairs of the gray squirrel. Their paper was made of bamboo, jute, and cotton. Nanha also painted on silk.

Georgia O'Keeffe
1887–1986

Georgia O'Keeffe (jôr´ jə ō kēf´) was born in Sun Prairie, Wisconsin. At the age of ten she began taking private art lessons, but the thing she liked most was experimenting with art at home. By 13, she had decided to become an artist. She trained under experts and won many prizes for her art. For years she challenged the art world with her unique vision. She eventually became famous for her spectacular, larger-than-life paintings of natural objects, including flowers, animal skulls, and shells. She loved nature, especially the desert of New Mexico, where she spent the last half of her life. O'Keeffe was married to the famous American photographer Alfred Stieglitz and appears in many of his photographs. In 1997, a Georgia O'Keeffe Museum opened in Santa Fe, New Mexico. It is the first museum in the United States devoted exclusively to the work of a major female artist.

About Art History

Stieglitz promoted modern artists and photographers from Europe and America through a magazine called *Camera Work* and a gallery known as "291." O'Keeffe and the circle of artists she met through Stieglitz were pioneers of modernism in the United States. She took subjects into her imagination and altered and simplified their appearances. She expressed her emotions through her vivid paintings.

About the Artwork

O'Keeffe's artwork features bold, colorful, abstract patterns and shapes. She most often painted natural forms such as flowers and bleached bones, pulling them out of their usual environments. She never painted portraits but sometimes painted landscapes.

About the Media

O'Keeffe used oils and watercolors for her paintings. She used pastels, charcoal, and pencil for her drawings.

About the Technique

O'Keeffe worked in dazzling, jewel-toned colors. She chose unusual perspectives, such as very close up or far away. She also enlarged the scale of her subjects.

Pablo Picasso
1881–1973

Pablo Picasso (pä´ blō pi kä´ sō) was born in Málaga, Spain. He did poorly in school but his father, an art teacher, taught him to draw and paint. Picasso learned quickly. When he was only 14 he had a painting accepted for an exhibition. Picasso moved to Paris, France when he was 18. At the time he was very poor. Thieves stole what little he had, yet they left his now valuable drawings. In time the outgoing Picasso made many friends. Among them were the American writers Ernest Hemingway and Gertrude Stein and the Russian composer Igor Stravinsky. Picasso painted at night and slept late most mornings. He worked hard his entire life. He completed 200 paintings the year he turned 90.

About Art History

Picasso was one of the most influential artists of the 1900s. He experimented with many styles and created new ones. He invented the style known as cubism. He took 18 months to paint his first cubist picture, *Les Demoiselles d'Avignon,* which shows five women from several angles. Other artists were soon copying his style.

About the Artwork

Picasso's paintings changed as his life changed. When he was poor, he painted sad pictures in shades of blue. This style is called his *Blue Period.* When he fell in love with a neighbor, he painted happier pictures in shades of pink. This style is called his *Rose Period.* Then came his cubist period, and later he painted in a style that reminded viewers of Greek sculpture.

About the Media

Picasso created drawings, oil paintings, ceramic pieces, sculptures, prints, and engravings. He also invented collage along with the French artist Georges Braque. They combined colored papers, newspaper, old illustrations, and small objects with painting and drawing to produce collages.

About the Technique

In his cubist paintings, Picasso simplified his subjects into circles, triangles, and other basic shapes. He often outlined these shapes in black or a bright color.

Paul Jackson Pollock

1912–1956

Paul Jackson Pollock (pôl jak´sən pä´lək) was born in Cody, Wyoming, but spent his childhood in Arizona and California. He first studied painting in Los Angeles, California, at Manual Arts High School and then moved to New York City to study under Thomas Hart Benton at the Art Students League. Pollock next worked with the Mexican muralist David Alfaro Siqueiros, from whom he learned unusual painting techniques. Pollock's solo show at the Guggenheim's Art of this Century Gallery in 1943 led to a contract with the gallery that allowed him to spend all his time painting. In 1945 he married artist Lee Krasner. Pollock died in an alcohol-related accident 11 years later.

About Art History

Pollock's early work was influenced by Picasso and surrealist artists. Along with artists such as Mark Rothko and Willem de Kooning, he was a central figure in the abstract expressionist movement. This art style focuses on pure expression through the use of form and color; the artwork does not represent anything recognizable. Pollock's art pushed America to the forefront of the modern art world.

About the Artwork

Although Pollock created paintings in other styles, such as surrealistic, his most famous works incorporated an abstract expressionistic style. Rather than making art meant to tell stories or imitate nature, Pollock created paintings that expressed his feelings; he did not intend for them to have concrete messages.

About the Media

Pollock used oil paints, sometimes mixed with other media such as glass, sand, charcoal, pastels, or gouache.

About the Technique

Pollock generally painted on loose canvases spread on the floor or tacked to walls. Rather than using brushes to apply paint, he used objects such as sticks and trowels to drip and fling paint onto the canvas. Pollock chose not to work from sketches; he tried to work spontaneously to give each painting a life of its own.

Diego Rivera
1886–1957

Diego Rivera (dē ā´ gō rē bā´ rä) was one of the most productive Mexican artists. He attended art school in Mexico but did not stay long. His first exhibition of paintings in 1907 won him a scholarship to Europe. There he studied the work of modern artists. After returning from a second trip to Europe in 1911, he became Mexico's leading mural painter. Rivera was a large man with strong opinions. His great love for his people and his country showed in his art. Crowds gathered to watch him paint his large murals on public walls. His third wife was the famous painter Frida Kahlo. They often fought and separated, but they always supported each other's artistic efforts.

About Art History

Rivera's painting style was influenced by the work of Klee, Cézanne, Picasso, and pre-Columbian, ancient Mexican art. He wanted to create art that could be enjoyed and understood by ordinary people. For this reason, Rivera focused on simple designs and interesting subjects. Public murals were ideal for him because many people could see his work.

About the Artwork

Rivera painted more than two-and-a-half miles of murals in Mexico, California, Michigan, and New York. For a huge stairway at the National Palace in Mexico City, Mexico, Rivera painted 124 panels. The panels trace the history of Mexico. In his other murals, Rivera often showed peasants working or celebrating.

About the Media

Rivera completed about 300 *frescoes,* which are paintings on fresh, moist plaster. He also painted on canvas with oils and watercolors.

About the Technique

For his frescoes, Rivera drew his designs on damp plaster and then copied them onto transparent paper. If the plaster dried out before Rivera could complete the painting, his assistant used the paper to re-create the designs on the wall.

John Robinson
1912–1995

American painter John Robinson (jän rä´ bin sən) is known for his scenes of African American community and family life. He first began painting when he was a child and had time to work on his art only after school. When he quit school to help support his family, Robinson continued to pursue art and painted during the little spare time he had between his many jobs. In 1929 he moved to Anacostia, in southeastern Washington, D.C., and immediately began to create paintings using the community as his subject.

▲ **John Robinson.** (American).
Here, Look at Mine. 1980.

Acrylic on canvas. $37\frac{1}{2} \times 26\frac{1}{2}$ inches (95.25 × 67.31 cm.). The Anacostia Museum on Center for African American History and Culture, Washington, D.C.

About Art History

Anacostia was recognized for its active arts community during the early and mid-1900s. Robinson's involvement with this movement began when he was helping his grandfather work at a garage, where he came into contact with people connected with important members of Washington's African American artistic community. Two professors, James V. Herring and James A. Porter, gave Robinson painting instruction and helped him begin his artistic career.

About the Artwork

Intimate scenes of family and community life characterize Robinson's art. His compositions often involve two or more people situated in a picture plane that opens up to the viewer. In pieces such as *Mr. and Mrs. Barton* and *Here, Look at Mine,* spaces left open or extended to the front of the composition invite viewers to step into the paintings. Robinson was talented at portraying the personality of his subjects and at capturing their individual traits.

About the Media

Robinson worked with oil and acrylic paints. He also created public murals for churches and along city streets.

About the Technique

Robinson referenced live models and sketches for his large-scale paintings. His street paintings reference actual urban locations that he would visit and study in order to capture specific detail.

George Segal
1924–2000

Not long before George Segal (jorj sē´ gəl) was born, his parents emigrated from eastern Europe to the Bronx in New York. They did not consider art to be a legitimate profession, but Segal insisted on studying art in college. After graduating in 1947, he started a chicken farm in New Jersey and taught at a high school to support his wife and two children. In 1958, he sold his chickens and used the buildings the chickens were housed in as his studio. For the next two years he created plaster figures on wood and chicken wire frames. All the art teachers in that area received surplus gauze embedded with plaster from a nearby Johnson & Johnson plant to give to Segal. He used this gauze to create his sculptures.

While teaching an art class in 1961, he hit upon the idea of making a plaster cast of his own body, removing the cast, and placing the hollow figure in a real-life setting.

About Art History

Segal's combination of painting and sculpture helped bridge the gap between abstract expressionism and pop art. He was influenced by Degas, Mondrian, Cézanne, and Picasso.

About the Artwork

Segal created scenes that focus on human relationships, such as the lonely figures in *The Gas Station* or *The Diner*. Segal drew attention to human events such as the civil rights movement and the Vietnam conflict. Some of his pieces have been controversial, such as *Kent State: Abraham and Isaac*. Although Kent State University asked Segal to create a monument to honor the demonstrators who were killed there, the university did not accept his finished work because it showed the violence about to be committed. This sculpture finally found a home at Princeton University in Princeton, New Jersey.

About the Media

At first, Segal used ordinary plaster to form his figures. In 1971, he switched to a more durable industrial plaster called *hydrostone.* Later he began casting sculptures in bronze.

About the Technique

Segal later formed his figures by wrapping a model in plaster-soaked bandages and removing them after they hardened. He placed his white plaster people into complex settings with real objects. He created a diner, a gas station, a street corner, and butcher shop, and then created an eerie effect by placing his stark-white plaster people with colorful real objects.

Charles Sheeler
1883–1965

Charles Sheeler (chärlz shē´ lər), an American painter and photographer, was born in Philadelphia, Pennsylvania. He entered the Pennsylvania School of Industrial Art in 1900. He studied classical art and ornamentation. Sheeler began studying art at the famous Pennsylvania Academy of Fine Arts in 1903 and learned to paint there. Around 1906, he became friends with Morton Schamberg, a former architecture student from the University of Pennsylvania. The two shared a studio in Philadelphia where they often discussed modern French painting. These discussions were important to Sheeler. He traveled in Europe from 1908 to 1909 and studied the works of French painters. In 1919 Sheeler moved to New York City. The urban life and architecture inspired Sheeler's art.

▲ **Charles Sheeler.** (American). *Self Portrait.* 1924.

Pastel on paper. $22\frac{1}{4} \times 19$ inches (58.4 × 48.2 cm.).
National Portrait Gallery, Smithsonian Institution, Washington, D. C.

About Art History

Sheeler was influenced by the highly structured works of Cézanne and also by the cubists. Gradually he developed a unique personal style that was precise. He and his contemporaries questioned the separation of fine art from crafts. Fine art was said to be taught at art schools and universities, whereas crafts included ordinary objects. By creating works of art from these objects, Sheeler and his contemporaries helped bridge the gap between fine art and crafts.

About the Artwork

Sheeler was famous for painting and photographing industry, architecture, and everyday objects. He created naturalistic scenes as well as abstract, industrial scenes in which he arranged the hard-edged forms of machinery into abstract patterns.

About the Media

Sheeler practiced painting, drawing, and photography. His drawings were done with conté crayon on paper. He painted with oils on canvas, tempera on board, and watercolors on paper. His photographs were gelatin silver prints.

About the Technique

Sheeler used colors and lines to create rhythmic patterns. Light was also important in Sheeler's art. His style evolved to become hard-edged and tightly organized.

Jaune Quick-to-See Smith

b. 1941

Jaune Quick-to-See Smith (zhōn kwik tōō sē smith) was born into a large family on a Montana reservation. She often went hungry as a child. Her Shoshone grandmother gave her the name "Quick-to-See" because Smith was quick to understand things. When Smith was in first grade, she already knew she wanted to be an artist. Later she was told that she was not college material and that a woman could not have a career in art. Smith spent 22 years supporting herself, raising three children, finishing college, and completing a master's degree in painting. She now paints as frequently as possible in a remodeled stable behind her home in New Mexico. When she is not painting, she lectures, teaches, and serves as a guest artist at colleges across the nation. Smith has been featured in magazines and several documentaries.

About Art History

Smith combines techniques used by abstract expressionist painters with images from her Native American background. Some galleries rejected Smith's modern paintings because they were not "Indian enough." For this reason, Smith arranges regular exhibits for young Native American artists. She wants these artists to be able to exhibit their work no matter what their subjects include.

About the Artwork

Smith's work expresses her concern about the destruction of the environment and of Native American cultures. In *Forest,* for example, a real handsaw in the painting suggests the future destruction of trees. In *Trade Gifts for Trading Land with White People,* she combined real souvenirs from sports teams that were named using Native American terms such as *Braves* and *Indians.* To Smith, the souvenirs and team names show a lack of respect for Native American cultures.

About the Media

Smith most frequently integrates real objects, such as ropes, nails, and spoons, and oil paints.

About the Technique

Smith adds texture to her paintings by pasting pieces of fabric and paper onto the canvas and painting over them. She blends colors with her hand.

Tony Smith
1912–1980

Tony Smith (tō´ nē smith) was born in New Jersey, the grandson of a designer and the son of an engineer. Although he grew up among builders, his artistic talent had a traumatic beginning. When he was four, he contracted tuberculosis and was forced to live alone in a little prefabricated house in his backyard. He lived there for a few years so his family would not be exposed to his germs. It was in this tiny quarantined space that he first modeled small pueblos like those he had seen at a World's fair and took his first steps toward a career in architectural sculpture.

▲ **Tony Smith.** (American). *Gracehoper.* 1971.
Welded steel and paint. Height 23 feet (7 m.).
The Detroit Institute of Arts, Detroit, Michigan.

About Art History

Smith studied and worked with the architect Frank Lloyd Wright in the late 1930s, and many of his earlier designs for houses can be attributed to Wright's influence. Architecture was not Smith's true calling, however, the larger building he had designed was never constructed. In 1953, his wife's opera career took her to Europe, and he accompanied her, bringing his sketchbooks and his hope for inspiration. He found it in a pattern of circles in a grid that he called the *Louisenberg* series. Once back in the United States, Smith began using these designs in abstract, architectural sculptures, many of which rigidly reflect the organic American sentiment of Henry David Thoreau and Walt Whitman. He was a contemporary of and friends with the abstract expressionist artists Jackson Pollock and Mark Rothko.

About the Artwork

The mammoth steel sculptures for which Smith is known are often two or more stories high and demonstrate his geometric background in architecture.

About the Media

Many of Smith's sculptures are made of black steel.

About the Technique

Smith had construction assistants help him assemble his huge multiton sculptures and weld them together. He would begin an idea for a sculpture by sketching a system of nets and grids, and then slowly form a three-dimensional plan based on these designs. His giant pieces of art often took years to create.

Frank Stella
b. 1936

Frank Stella (frangk ste´lə) was born in Malden, Massachusetts, in 1936. He studied painting at Phillips Academy and majored in history at Princeton University. He supported himself after college by painting houses. He moved to New York City, where he had his first successful show called *Sixteen Americans*. At the age of 23, he was the youngest artist in the show. At first people were annoyed and shocked by his style. However, his talent was noticed by a few important gallery owners and critics who felt his work was exciting and new. Later in his life he became an architect.

About Art History

Stella began to paint at the end of the influential period of abstract expressionism. He is not an emotional painter like Jackson Pollock. Instead, Stella wants to paint *essential art.* This means reducing painting to strict geometric designs. He belonged to a group of artists called the "hard-edge" painters. This group used geometric shapes and little color in their works.

About the Artwork

Stella's first exhibited works were black pinstripe paintings. This style paved the way for minimalism. In the 1960s he experimented with bright colors and oddly-shaped canvases. He produced many series of paintings. One of the best known is the *protractor series,* which is made of large circles, half circles, and bright colors. In the late 1970s he combined his earlier expressionistic style with three-dimensional canvases that project nearly two feet toward the viewer's face.

About the Media

Stella uses oils, sometimes with a metallic finish. In building huge, painted canvases, he uses wood to prop up his paintings.

About the Technique

Stella's work is painted freehand. He begins by drawing guidelines on the canvas. He then fills in the space between the lines with paint. He leaves the white canvas showing between bands of paint. Sometimes he uses canvases in *U* and *L* shapes.

Paul Strand

1890–1976

Paul Strand (pôl strand) was born in New York City to a middle-class family. He was educated at the Ethical Cultural School where practical skills, including photography, were taught. After graduating from high school, Strand learned more about photography from the New York Camera Club, a local hobby league. He traveled around America and Mexico taking pictures and developing his style. He moved to Europe in the 1950s and traveled through parts of Africa in the 1960s.

About Art History

Strand's early photography followed the style of Alfred Stieglitz's Photo-Secession group. This group took photographs that looked like soft drawings and paintings. He spent some time experimenting with photographic modernism, a style influenced by the pictorialism and cubist painting styles, before settling into a more formal style.

About the Artwork

Strand experimented with camera angles in many of his early photographs and learned how to "build" a picture. His early portraits show the personalities of different people. He also photographed machines, an unusual concept for the time. Strand is best known for his humanistic portraits and landscapes that carry social messages. After 1917, his photographs became less experimental.

About the Media

Strand often printed his pictures on platinum paper, which made the images look crisp and clear.

About the Technique

For a time Strand used a camera with a false lens so the subjects of his portraits would not look directly into the true lens. He also experimented with cubist photography, in which he would take pictures of a still life from many different angles.

Louis Sullivan
1856–1924

Louis Henri Sullivan (lōō´ əs sə´ lə vən) was born in Boston, Massachusetts, and grew up with his grandparents in South Reading, Massachusetts. When he was 16 he attended the Massachusetts Institute of Technology, where he studied architecture with some of America's leading draftsmen. His work led him to Chicago, where he designed numerous city buildings and became involved with the country's early creation of skyscrapers.

About Art History

At MIT, Sullivan studied under architects William Ware and Eugene Letang, and he worked with Frank Furness and William LeBaron Jenney. He then traveled to Paris and briefly attended the École des Beaux-Arts before returning to the United States. He arrived in Chicago just as the city was starting to be rebuilt following the Chicago fire of 1871 and joined a partnership with the architect Dankmar Adler. These two men produced many buildings at the cutting edge of American architecture and skyscraper design and were mentors to the young Frank Lloyd Wright, who joined their firm in 1888. In 1895, Sullivan ended his partnership with Adler and began creating smaller buildings in small towns. He also wrote books on organic architecture, stressing the importance of the connection between architecture and the human experience with nature.

About the Artwork

Sullivan believed that a form's ornamental design was just as important as its function, and his buildings and drawings were full of impressive ornamental details. In his plans and projects Sullivan attempted to reconcile the world of nature with the world of science and technology, and his architectural style often referenced organic and natural forms.

About the Media

Sullivan used many materials, both on the exterior and interior of his buildings. In *Chicago Auditorium* he incorporated brick, terra-cotta, marble, fine wood, gilding, glass-mosaic, and tinted window glass.

About the Technique

To create proposals for a building, Sullivan made hundreds of drawings of the planned interior and exterior. He used these drawings to explore all possible options and combinations of materials.

Judith Surowiec

b. 1938

Judith Surowiec (jōō´ dith sûr ō´ ic) was born in Buffalo, New York, and grew up in a creative family. She began drawing at an early age and was encouraged by her mother to pursue creative activities. Surowiec and her family even made their own toys. She became interested in art when she encountered the watercolor paintings of her elementary art teacher, Ms. Valentine. Surowiec knew then that she wanted to study art, and she now provides a similar experience for young students by visiting classes and helping them feel excited about creativity. Surowiec lives and works in Georgia.

About Art History

Surowiec studied art at the State University of New York and graduated with a degree in art education. She did not have the time to teach in public school, however, because she married and started a family shortly after graduating. Surowiec continued to paint in her spare time and became skilled in creating realistic portraits based on photographs. Viewers and collectors admired and supported this work, but Surowiec believed that her strict adherence to photographic references limited her artistic creativity. A 1986 painting class with teacher Joe Perrin in Atlanta, Georgia, brought about a change and helped her develop an intuitive creativity and freedom.

About the Artwork

Surowiec paints from her soul. She claims, "If you know what you're doing or where you're going, you're not being creative." Surowiec created the painting *Art Teacher* in 1996 while she visited an elementary school. The students contributed suggestions and ideas to Surowiec as she painted, and she included those suggestions in the final composition.

About the Media

Vibrant acrylic paints and colored pencil are Surowiec's most frequently used media.

About the Technique

Surowiec uses acrylic because it dries quickly and forces her to mix new colors throughout a composition. Acrylic also allows her to do something new each time and to add many layers of paint in a short period of time. After starting a painting on location Surowiec returns to her studio where she can slow down her pace. Colored pencils allow her to create at a more relaxing pace, and she prefers to draw with pencil at the end of the day as a winding-down technique. Sometimes she uses a crumpled canvas which makes the textures and colors of her work unique.

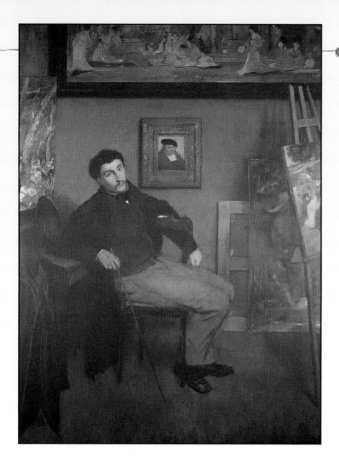

James Tissot
1836–1902

James Tissot (jāmz tē sō´) was born in France. His parents earned a profitable living making clothing for wealthy customers. This background later led Tissot to paint scenes of stylish women. As a youth, Tissot was sent away to attend religious schools, where he spent much of his time sketching his surroundings. Later he attended art school in Paris, where he became friends with Edgar Degas and other artists. His first exhibition in Paris was not a great success. Eventually, however, his artwork made him wealthy. During the Franco-Prussian War, Tissot fled from Paris to London, England, where he continued his career. Tissot never married.

▲ **Edgar Degas.** (French).
Portrait of James Tissot. 1867–1868.

Oil on canvas. $59\frac{5}{8} \times 44$ inches (151.4 × 112 cm.).
The Metropolitan Museum of Art, New York, New York.

About Art History

A practical man, Tissot was more concerned with pleasing his customers than with developing his artistic skills. Still he is probably better appreciated as an artist today than he was during his lifetime. Art critics credit him with accurately recording the mood of the Victorian era. Tissot was one of the first artists to use photos to archive his paintings. He also based some of his paintings on photographs.

About the Artwork

Early in his career Tissot painted scenes with well-dressed women who seemed lonely or bored. Later he painted biblical scenes, which were popular during his lifetime. *The Prodigal Son in Modern Life* is probably the best known and is set in medieval surroundings.

About the Media

Along with his oil paintings, watercolors, and etchings, Tissot worked in enamels and sculpture.

About the Technique

Toward the end of his career Tissot often made copies of his paintings. The copies are sometimes smaller versions or the same scene reproduced as watercolors or etchings.

George Tooker
b. 1920

George Tooker (jorj tōōk´ ər) grew up in Brooklyn and Long Island, New York. His family was part of the upper class, and this upbringing is reflected in his paintings. He gained an understanding of a genteel lifestyle—as well the lifestyle of those who were less privileged—and he became interested in the use of art as a tool for social change. Tooker considers himself to be a reporter and he creates compositions that reflect his views of everyday life.

About Art History

While majoring in English at Harvard University, Tooker became inspired by the Mexican muralists David Siqueiros and Jose Orozco. In 1943, he began taking classes at the Art Students League in New York where he studied with Reginald Marsh and Kenneth Hayes Miller. He was friends with the artist Paul Cadmus, who encouraged him to work in egg tempera. Tooker's work was recognized with that of Edward Hopper, Andrew Wyeth, Jared French, and other American realists whose paintings evoked a spiritual alienation and personal uncertainty during the Cold War era. While painting in the 1950s, Tooker became famous for unsettling depictions of the isolation and anonymity of urban life.

About the Artwork

Critics have referred to Tooker's style as *magic realism,* with its characteristic hint at surrealism. His subjects often have mixed features, and appear to sag in their own bodies. In *Bird Watchers* Tooker wanted to create a positive piece with religious undertones but no religious subject matter. His simplified and standardized subjects suggest the

Crucifixion as they represent the figures of Mary, Mary Magdelene, the apostles, and soldiers. They are not biblical figures, however. Instead they are people set in the 1940s era with a timeless appearance to their stiff postures.

About the Media

Egg tempera is a type of paint made by mixing an egg yolk with water and then adding powdered pigment to the mix. The result of this process is a paint that dries very quickly and is hard to change once it is applied. Many Italian Renaissance painters used egg tempera. Egg tempera's fast drying rate requires the artist to paint confidently and steadily, beginning at one end of the canvas and working toward the other without layering or erasing.

About the Technique

Tooker completes only about two paintings per year because he spends a great deal of time brainstorming and sketching ideas for his compositions.

Henri de Toulouse-Lautrec

1864–1901

Henri de Toulouse-Lautrec (än rē´ də tōō lōōz´ lō trek´) was born in France. He stopped growing after his legs were injured in a childhood accident. He spent much of his brief adult life in clubs and music halls in Paris. Scenes from these places became favorite subjects of his paintings. Toulouse-Lautrec fought an addiction to alcohol during his life, and he died at the age of 37.

About Art History

Toulouse-Lautrec was influenced by the French impressionist painter Degas, who painted soft, flowing pictures of ballet dancers and women bathing. The impressionists were interested in the effects of light on surfaces. But unlike the work of most impressionists, Toulouse-Lautrec's paintings were often dark and mysterious. They expressed how he felt about life and his environment. This idea of expressing the artist's feelings was adopted by a later group of artists called *expressionists.* Toulouse-Lautrec also created lithographic posters to advertise events at the Moulin Rouge, a club in Paris. These posters were pulled off advertising kiosks and saved by art collectors.

About the Artwork

Toulouse-Lautrec painted circuses, dancers, and sportsmen, and he used dark, unnatural colors. One of his famous paintings, *At the Moulin Rouge,* shows a scene of people in a club. The picture is not centered on the canvas, which is a characteristic of Toulouse-Lautrec's style.

About the Media

Toulouse-Lautrec generally worked in oils on canvas, although he sometimes painted on cardboard. He created the first lithographic posters, which were considered masterpieces of printmaking. He was so concerned about the quality of the posters that he mixed his own colors of ink for the printer.

About the Technique

Many of Toulouse-Lautrec's paintings seem haunting or frightening because he painted people's faces with strange colors, such as green or purple. The faces are also lit from unusual angles, making the people seem as though they are wearing masks. To achieve this effect, Toulouse-Lautrec used light colors under the chins, noses, and eyebrows.

Jørn Oberg Utzon
b. 1918

This Danish architect first learned about building from his father, a noted yacht designer. Jørn Oberg Utzon (jorn ō´ burg ut´ zən) studied at the Royal Academy of Art in Denmark. He first gained international recognition in 1957, when his design for the Opera House in Sydney, Australia, was selected from 223 entries. Utzon moved to Australia to oversee the construction. However, major delays and disagreements with local politicians forced Utzon to resign, and another architect oversaw the construction. Since then Utzon has continued to design unusual buildings. An example is a church in Copenhagen that looks like a cluster of farm buildings.

About Art History

Utzon has led the way in designing modern buildings that are romantic and expressive. His work is influenced by his study of nature and of Islamic and Asian architecture. He also worked with architects Gunnar Asplund and Alvar Aalto and admires the designs of Frank Lloyd Wright and Ludwig Mies van der Rohe. Utzon invented the term *additive architecture,* a form of architecture in which components are joined to form a whole.

About the Artwork

Utzon's Opera House in Sydney has two parts: the seating areas called the podium and the graceful concrete shells that seem to float above everything. These two parts are joined with glass walls that give visitors a feeling of openness. Utzon's other projects range from a housing development in Denmark to a bank in Iran.

About the Media

Utzon was one of the first to use standard, mass-produced materials to produce complex structures.

About the Technique

Utzon always designs his buildings, including the Sydney Opera House, to blend with their surroundings. He prefers wide, horizontal lines, like those in ancient Mayan and Aztec architecture.

▲ **Vincent van Gogh.** (Dutch).
Self-Portrait with a Straw Hat. 1885.

Oil on canvas. 16 × 12½ inches (40.6 × 31.8 cm.).
The Metropolitan Museum of Art, New York, New York.

Vincent van Gogh
1853–1890

Even as a boy in the Netherlands, Vincent van Gogh (vin´ sənt van gō´) cared about other people very much. He tried many jobs, including being a teacher, minister, and social worker. However, he had problems getting along with nearly everyone except his younger brother, Theo. At the age of 28, van Gogh decided that the best way he could serve others was through art. He expressed his deep feelings about people through his paintings. As he moved from place to place, he left many of his works behind. Some were burned in fireplaces for heat, and some were even used to patch holes in walls. Van Gogh was poor his entire life and often went hungry so that he could buy painting supplies. He died at age 37.

About Art History

Even though van Gogh sold only one painting in his lifetime, he is now considered the greatest nineteenth-century Dutch artist. He was one of the first to express his feelings through painting. This new school of art is now called *expressionism*.

About the Artwork

Van Gogh painted many different subjects, from portraits to landscapes. He once lived in France near fields of golden wheat and sunflowers, which he painted many times. He wrote that his sunflowers symbolized his gratitude toward others, especially his brother, who was one of the few people who encouraged him to paint.

About the Media

During the ten short years that van Gogh worked, he created hundreds of oil paintings, along with many drawings in ink, crayon, chalk, and charcoal.

About the Technique

Van Gogh wanted to show energy and motion in his work. He often put complementary colors, such as red and green, next to each other to add power to his paintings. He applied oil paints in thick layers, sometimes straight from the tubes. His thick layers, slashing brushstrokes, and swirling shapes give his paintings strong patterns that reflect his strong feelings.

▲ **Jan Vermeer.** (Dutch).
Detail from *At the Procuress.* 1656.

Oil on canvas. $56\frac{3}{4} \times 51\frac{1}{8}$ inches (143×130 cm.).
The Dresden State Art Collection, Dresden, Germany.

Jan Vermeer
1632–1675

Jan Vermeer (yän vər merʹ) was a Dutch painter born in Delft. Little is known about his life; he married at the age of 21 and was the father of 11 children. Vermeer served a six-year apprenticeship and was admitted to the Delft painters guild in 1653. He made a modest living as an art dealer running a business that was left to him by his father. No records have been found to show that he sold any of his own works. Forgotten for almost 200 years, Vermeer is now regarded as one of the greatest painters of all time. This is remarkable because only 35 of his paintings are known to exist. This small number of works is attributed to his deliberate, methodical work habits, his short life, and the disappearance of many of his paintings during the period of obscurity following his death.

About Art History

Like other Dutch artists of the seventeenth century, Vermeer painted genre scenes, landscapes, and portraits. This was different from most artwork produced in southern Europe at the time, which was primarily religious.

About the Artwork

Dutch genre painting reached its peak with Vermeer's work. He could capture a moment of life with all action seeming to cease. Vermeer masterfully depicted light and space. He usually used his wife and children as models.

About the Media

Vermeer painted with oils on canvas or wood backgrounds.

About the Technique

Vermeer was a master of optical reality. He included only the details that would be seen from a distance. His use of color and value was also consistent with what someone would actually see. He painted slowly and painstakingly, completing only two or three works a year. The textures of his painted objects are so realistic that the viewer is tempted to touch the surface to see how it feels.

Elon Webster

Elon Webster (e´lən web´stər) was an Onondaga carver who lived on the Tonawanda Reservation in New York during the early part of the twentieth century. *Iroquois* is a collective name for the Mohawk, Oneida, Onondaga, Cayaga, and Senaca tribes, groups that speak Iroquois-related languages and have similar cultures. Webster worked for the Works Progress Administration (WPA) on the Seneca Arts Project during the 1930s.

About Art History

Elon Webster was one of 100 artists who produced works of art under the Seneca Arts Project, a specialized program initiated by Authur A. Parker, director of the Rochester Museum, that promoted Native American Arts. This program not only provided work for victims of the Great Depression, but also encouraged pride and community cooperation. Although the group of artists successfully produced works of art based on traditional Iroquios arts and crafts, the goal of creating permanent positions for artists never materialized. Elon Webster was one of the most successful artists among the group and is known for his mask production.

About the Artwork

To the Iroquois, masks are important symbols of spiritual forces that affect their lives and well-being. Frequently, stories accompany the masks to explain why they possess certain qualities. Elon Webster's mask represents the *fire man*, or *old broken-nose*, whose nose was injured by a moving mountain in a contest of power. His twisted mouth symbolizes that he is blowing hot ashes.

About the Media

Many Iroquois masks were made from basswood, which is light, strong, and easily carved. White horsetail, sheet copper, and red barn paint, in addition to animal hair, clamshells, and earth pigments, were used to create and decorate the masks.

About the Technique

Webster's modern mask is more sophisticated than earlier masks. Earlier masks were created by using the rounded outside surface of a tree for the face. The hollowed-out wood had holes burned into place for the eyes. Different decorations were added to make each mask unique. Sometimes wrinkles were carved into the forehead, metal plates were positioned for eye holes, or hair was attached to the top of the mask.

James McNeill Whistler
1834–1903

Although James McNeill Whistler (jāmz mək nēl´ hwis´ lər) was born in Lowell, Massachusetts, he often claimed that he was born somewhere in Europe. Whistler did spend part of his childhood in Russia— his father, an engineer, helped construct the St. Petersburg-Moscow railroad—and he studied at the Imperial Academy of Fine Arts for one year. After returning to America, Whistler attended West Point Military Academy, and then he traveled to Paris to study art. Throughout his career Whistler worked experimentally and refused to be associated with any one style of painting.

▲ **James McNeill Whistler.** (American).
Arrangement in Gray: Portrait of the Painter. c. 1872.

Oil on canvas. 29 × 21 inches (74.9 × 53.3 cm.).
The Detroit Institute of Arts, Detroit, Michigan.

About Art History

When Whistler first went to Paris, the city's artists were divided between traditional styles and the radical ideas of artists, such as Courbet, who said artists should paint what seems relevant. Whistler painted at the studio of Charles Gleyre, where he was encouraged to experiment. In 1859, Whistler moved to London where he was influenced by the *pre-Raphaelites,* a group of English artists who wished to recapture the beauty of the medieval world, and the *impressionists,* who felt that artists should paint directly from nature. He strongly believed in the aesthetic principle of creating art for its own sake.

About the Artwork

Whistler painted many outdoor scenes and portraits, but for much of his life he insisted that an artwork's subject did not matter. He believed his art should be aesthetically pleasing and not emotionally charged. Whistler is best known for his paintings and drawings, but he also designed color schemes for rooms and decorated furniture and houses.

About the Media

Whistler used oil paints, watercolors, pen and ink, and pastels.

About the Technique

As Whistler moved away from realism toward a more aesthetic style, he began to use thinner layers of paint and fewer colors in his paintings. Whistler sometimes used a Parisian "memory method," by which he would study a scene and draw it from memory. Later he chose to paint directly from nature.

Richard Yarde

b. 1939

Richard Yarde (ri´ chərd yärd) was born in Boston and lives in Northampton, Massachusetts. Yarde's bright energetic watercolors have earned him national acclaim. His work can be found in more than 30 public collections. In 1991 Yarde became ill with a life-threatening kidney ailment that caused him to temporarily lose the sense of touch in his right hand. In order to fully heal he used his artwork as therapy for both his physical and emotional condition, and he created a body of work that addressed his illness and humankind's mortality. He has been a professor of art at the University of Massachusetts at Amherst since 1990.

About Art History

Since the 1960s, Yarde has created powerful watercolors in the New England art world. He has used his art to depict cultural symbols, such as African American heroes, and dance, as an expression of his culture. His illness changed his art, which now addresses issues of mortality, vulnerability, healing, and rebirth. With Yarde's 1970s *Hero* series came a progression into his *Savoy* paintings, both of which were influenced by the vibrant jazz culture of the Harlem Renaissance.

About the Artwork

Music and dance are important to Yarde. His Savoy Ballroom paintings were directly inspired by the drama, joy, and risk-taking of the dancers, as well as the roots of African dance. *Savoy: Heel and Toe* expresses this joyful energy in its exciting composition and pulsing colors. Two people revolve in the picture plane, and the man's dancing feet and the woman's twirling skirt are caught in colorful motion. This painting depicts a single frozen moment during a dance. Yarde created

this series of paintings from 1940s *Life* magazine photographs.

About the Media

Yarde uses bold colors and powerful imagery in his watercolors. His involvement with installation art includes *Ringshout,* a piece named after and inspired by a religious ceremony and healing ritual practiced by African American slaves.

About the Technique

Watercolor is a delicate medium and requires careful application. Yarde makes sketches and studies of his compositions before sketching the final draft on heavy watercolor paper. A watercolor sketch is typically drawn lightly with a hard pencil. Some artists try to erase their pencil lines, and others prefer to leave the graphite on the paper as an added element. Watercolor pigment is mixed with water and applied in layers, with the deepest or most vibrant colors receiving the most layers.

Bowl

Potters of the Kongo people were traditionally women. Ceramic bowls such as this one were made for daily use in activities such as cooking, serving food, and holding water. Despite their mundane purposes, these bowls were often decorated with beautiful designs and colorful finish glazes, making them look more like unique works of art than everyday household objects.

▲ **Artist unknown.** (Kongo Peoples, Congo and Democratic Republic of the Congo). *Bowl.* Late-nineteenth to early twentieth century.

Ceramic and resin. $4\frac{1}{8} \times 5\frac{7}{8} \times 5\frac{7}{8}$ inches (10.5 × 14.9 × 14.9 cm.). Smithsonian Museum of African Art, Washington, D.C.

About Art History

During the late nineteenth and early twentieth centuries, Europeans became increasingly fascinated by African artwork. So many European visitors to the continent returned to Europe with works of African art that huge public and private collections could be viewed throughout Europe. Unfortunately, much of the art history of the Kongo people was lost as a result of the turbulent years of Portuguese and Belgian control and the removal of artwork by foreign collectors. This bowl was probably made during the period of Belgian colonial rule in the geographic area that is now the Democratic Republic of the Congo.

About the Artwork

Although some ceramic bowls were made by the Kongo people for use during ceremonies or as containers for offerings in shrines, this bowl was probably a common household vessel used to serve food.

About the Media

The heavy, dense clay soil of central Africa provides ample resources for the creation of many different types of ceramics. The finish is an example of one of the inventive ways Kongo people created paints and glazes with which to decorate their works.

About the Technique

This bowl was handformed from clay and then fired at a relatively low temperature. When the bowl was removed from the kiln, a special type of glaze made from tree bark was splattered onto its hot surface. As the bowl cooled, this glaze formed a delicate ring pattern as the liquid from the bark mixture slowly evaporated.

Ceremonial Panel

This ceremonial panel was made during the middle of the twentieth century by a small group of Kuba weavers of central Africa. The majority of Kuba people live in the Democratic Republic of the Congo, formerly called Zaire. The Congo is a mountainous, densely forested area. Its plentiful natural resources provide materials for Kuba works of basketry, woven textiles, sculpture, carvings, and many other types of art.

◄ **Artist unknown.** (Kuba Group, Western Kasai Province, Democratic Republic of Congo). *Ceremonial Panel.* c. 1950–1975.

Cut-pile and linear embroidery on plain-weave raffia palm. 22 × 23½ inches (55.88 × 59.69 cm.). Museum of International Folk Art, Santa Fe, New Mexico.

About Art History

The Kuba people are known for their use of bold, complex, asymmetrical patterns in the creation of their strikingly beautiful textiles. One interesting aspect of Kuba textile production is that entire families participate in the long process of making them.

About the Artwork

Raffia panels are worn by Kuba people during important ceremonies, such as funerals. Women and men use these panels as clothing, wrapping them around their waists to serve as skirts or sarongs. During funeral rituals, raffia panels are draped over the body and then buried with the deceased.

About the Media

Like most of the woven textiles produced by the Kuba peoples, this ceremonial panel is made of long fibers of the raphia vinifera palm, which grows in abundance in central Africa. This material is commonly called raffia. Embroidery thread and various dyes are also used in the stitching and decoration of Kuba *raffia* textiles. The artisans who create them exhibit their creativity and imagination through the intricate patterns they design for each individual panel.

About the Technique

Women and children gather and strip the raffia fibers to prepare them for weaving. Men are generally the weavers of the raffia, working on single heddle looms to produce sheets of the fibrous cloth. This cloth is then softened by soaking it in water and pounding it with a stone mortar. Patterns on the cloth are made by dying the raffia, cutting out sections and patching them onto different parts of the cloth, and by embellishing the finished cloth with patches of cotton fabric and elaborate stitching.

Deep Dish

There are no marks on this deep dish that identify the potter or workshop that created it. Although records exist that name masters of Valencian pottery, specific attribution to individual artists and their works is unknown. Potters of various religious and ethnic backgrounds worked together in Valencia.

◄ **Artist unknown.** (Spain). *Deep Dish.* 1430.
....
Tin-glazed earthenware painted in cobalt blue and lustre.
$2\frac{3}{5}$ inches × 19 inches (6.7 × 48.2 cm.).
Hispanic Society of America, New York, New York.

About Art History

The Arabs conquered Spain in the eighth century, and soon all of Mesopotamia, Persia, and North Africa was under Islamic control. In Spain, Christian and Islamic scholars, traders, and artists exchanged ideas freely until the mid-sixteenth century. A new tradition of ceramics emerged from the blending of the Spanish and Islamic understanding of clay, glazes, and fire.

About the Artwork

This deep dish, typical of dishes with flat centers and horizontal brims, was created around 1430. The coat of arms in the center of the artwork has been attributed to the Despujol family of Catalonia. Bands and pointed ovals surround the shield. The bands contain designs that imitate Arabic inscriptions in blue and gold. A large heraldic eagle is painted on the back of the dish.

About the Media

This deep dish is made from clay found in the area. The fired pottery was then covered with a tin-oxide glaze.

About the Technique

The fifteenth century potters of Valencia used a complex firing system to create this deep dish. Although the precise process to create the lustre glaze is unknown, it is likely that it was created from various mineral bases. Modern potters speculate that copper and silver oxides were combined with red ochre and vinegar to create lustre glazes. Cobalt mixed with silica produced a blue glaze. Iron, present in many other Valencian pieces, produced glazes that were tinted green.

Featherwork Neckpiece

The weavers of Incan society were mostly men. They traveled deep into the jungle to capture the exotic birds whose feathers they used in making ceremonial clothing.

◀ **Artist unknown (Incan).** (Peru). *Featherwork Neckpiece.* 1350–1476.

Cotton, feathers, beads. Late Intermediate Period: China style. $13\frac{1}{4} \times 11\frac{1}{2}$ inches (33.66 × 29.21 cm.). Dallas Museum of Art, Dallas, Texas.

About Art History

The Incan civilization flourished from the twelfth century to the beginning of the sixteenth century. At its height in the 1400s, the Incan empire stretched along two-thirds of the South American coastline from present-day Peru to Chile. The Inca had a highly developed culture. Even today their temples, palaces, and forts are still standing throughout the Andes mountain range in Peru. They were famous for their advanced road system that ran well over a thousand miles. However, the road system helped the Spanish conquer the Inca in the 1500s.

About the Artwork

Neckpieces such as this one were found by archaeologists in Incan burial graves hidden in the Andes Mountains. The Inca wrapped their dead in many layers of ornate cloth, sometimes as many as 60 layers. Because the Incan civilization stretched along the Pacific coast, they relied heavily on the ocean for survival. The images here show pelicans diving for ocean fish. The one large man and the two men with only their heads showing are casting nets to catch fish.

About the Media

The neckpiece includes parrot and macaw feathers, and small seashells.

About the Technique

There is no proof that Incan artists prepared a design before beginning a piece. Most likely they simply created the pattern as they worked. This artist first wove the frame of the cloth in wool on a small loom. Next the exotic bird feathers were sewn in rows over the wool. The images of the birds, men, and pelicans were stitched afterwards using blue wool yarn. Finally the artists carved small shell beads and attached them to the bottom of the wool cloth.

Half of a Tunic

The Wari people, originally from the Andes Mountain region of central Peru, founded an enormous empire that extended from present-day Ecuador in the north to the border of Chile in the south. It is estimated that the Wari Empire existed during the period between 600 A.D. and 1000 A.D. In spite of the absence of any written records about its history, much has been learned about the Wari culture from the many artifacts that have been found in central Peru.

◀ **Artist unknown.** (Wari culture, Peru). *Half of a Tunic.* 600–900 A.D.

Plain weave sections tie-dyed and recombined, alpaca.
77 × 31 inches (195.58 × 78.74 cm.).
Museum of International Folk Art, Santa Fe, New Mexico.

About Art History

People of the Andes Mountains have been recognized for their weaving skills for centuries. Textiles, such as capes, tunics, blankets, and hats, have been recovered from the ruins and burial sites of the Inca, Chavin, Moche, Nazca, and Wari cultures. Scientists are amazed by how well many of these pieces have withstood the effects of time, which is probably due to the durability of their fibers and the care with which they were constructed. The Wari people developed such sophisticated methods for dying wool that, although it is well over 1,000 years old, this tunic still possesses its original vibrant colors.

About the Artwork

This tunic provides a classic example of the interesting patterns, designs, and symbols incorporated into woven textiles by the Wari people. The colors and patterns woven into garments conveyed information about the wearer's family, profession, or social position within the community.

The Wari tunic shown here may have been made for a wealthy noble or community leader, since the alpaca fiber from which it was woven would likely have been beyond the means of many ordinary citizens.

About the Media

This textile was handwoven from alpaca wool that was dyed prior to the construction of the tunic. Alpaca wool, which is still used to weave cloth today, is a very soft, durable fiber similar to the wool of llamas and vicuña. Alpaca wool is generally more expensive than other types of wool and is prized for its fine, silky texture.

About the Technique

Because the pedal loom had not yet been introduced to the peoples of South America, this tunic must have been handwoven. Sections of the wool were dyed and then assembled into these colorful Wari shapes and patterns.

Huichol Bead Mask

This bead mask was made by an unknown artist of the Huichol Indian peoples of Santa Catarina in Jalisco, Mexico. The Huichol Indians, a cultural and ethnic group descended from the Aztecs, live in the mountainous central Mexican states of Jalisco and Nayarit. Huichol artists do not sign their artwork, which makes it very difficult to identify the artist who created a specific piece. Within local Huichol culture, however, an artist's identity can often be determined by other members of the community by observing the style, materials, and construction of the piece.

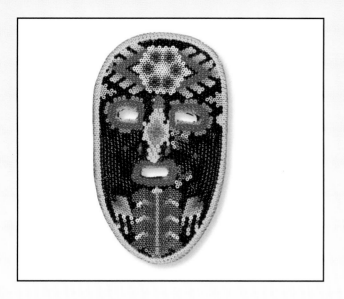

▲ **Artist unknown.** (Huichol People/Mexico). *Huichol Bead Mask.* 2000.

Wood and glass beads.
5 × 3 inches (12.7 × 7.62 cm.). Private collection.

About Art History

In Huichol culture people see themselves as mirrors of the gods. The Huichol believe that a person must look through and beyond the physical world to see the grand design of life. Masks are decorated with the same patterns and designs that the Huichol peoples' faces are painted with during sacred Huichol ceremonies. The masks represent the faces of the people who wear them. They are not worn during the ceremonies.

About the Artwork

The Huichol are able to record images that come to them in visions and dreams brought about by participation in the ritual ceremonies through the creation of these masks. The masks are an important part of the mythological and cultural traditions of the Huichol. This bead mask exemplifies the classic pattern, style, and brilliant colors often seen in Huichol bead art.

About the Media

This bead mask was made using wood, natural adhesives, and colorful beads.

About the Technique

Most Huichol bead masks are carved from the wood of a locally grown tree called *parota*. After carving the details onto the mask, Huichol artists spread a sticky mixture of beeswax and pine pitch on its surface. Then with great care and patience the artists apply tiny beads one at a time until the ornate beadwork covers the entire surface of the mask. Because Huichol artists make each piece by hand without the aid of patterns, and because each represents its wearer, each mask is one of a kind.

Huipil Weaving

The ancient Mayan people lived in present-day Guatemala, Belize, and the western edges of Honduras and El Salvador, as well as in the Mexican states of Yucatan, Quintano Roo, Campeche, Chiapas, and Tabasco. Their civilization thrived from 700 B.C. to 900 A.D. They believed that time, space, and the physical world were connected to the supernatural world. Many Mayan gods were believed to be combinations of animals and humans. The Mayans built cities with terraced pyramids, temples, palaces, monuments, and courtyards. They also built extensive roadways that supported their trading economy.

◀ **Artist unknown (Mayan).**
Huipil Weaving. c. 1950.
....

Backstrap woven plain weave with supplementary-weft pattern, silk on cotton. 50 × 14½ inches (127 × 36.83 cm.). The Girard Foundation Collection, Museum of International Folk Art, Santa Fe, New Mexico.

About Art History

Mayan art represented the Mayans' religious beliefs, worldview, and language. During the classical Mayan civilization, a system of glyph writing was used. Glyphs were pictorial symbols used to record historic events, dates, and titles. The principle image of the middle period was the portrait of the ruler. The ruler might be shown wearing jade and his personally symbolic clothes. A belt with crossed bands might symbolize the sky. A ruler also might wear a loincloth apron with a sun mask, a black dress with a skull, or a headdress with heavenly and underworld symbols.

About the Artwork

It is rare for archaeologists to discover clothing from the Mayan civilization because the tropical climate deteriorates the pieces over time. Clothing is studied from representations in sculpture, painted murals, and ceramics. This Huipil (wē pēl´)was made by contemporary Mayan artists.

About the Media

Most Huipils are made from white and brown cotton, which grows in the Mayan territory.

About the Technique

Mayans make cloth by hand sewing and weaving. Women are usually responsible for weaving and making cloth. Embroideries and brocade are used to decorate Mayan cloth.

Kwele Face Mask

The Kwele tribe of Gabon is one of many ethnic groups living in the equatorial forest region of central Africa. Beginning about 3,000 years ago, the equatorial forest region was settled by farmers from various regions and ethnic groups. Although the equatorial forest region is rich in ethnic diversity, its people share cultural similarities and beliefs. One example of this is a common belief that the spirits of deceased family members are present among the living. Many of the people in this region believe that the spiritual power of ancestral relics can protect and benefit their communities.

◀ **Artist unknown.** (Gabon). *Kwele Face Mask.* 19th–20th century.

Wood, paint. 20 inches (52.7 cm.) tall.
The Metropolitan Museum of Art, New York, New York.

About Art History

In the tribal ceremonies of many traditional African communities, masks are believed to be inhabited by spirits, giving the masks great social and religious importance. The Kwele used wood and fiber materials to create abstract ceremonial masks. Masks like the one shown here were called *ekuk*. They represented forest spirits and children of the Beete cult, depicted as animals or as humans with animal-like features. These masks were used in Beete cult ceremonies that were performed to protect tribal villages from famine, disease, and war.

About the Artwork

This mask was used in funeral ceremonies to connect the viewer to the abstract world of the dead and the sacred. This mask is mostly flat, with a human-like face surrounded by downward-curving animal horns. Like many masks created by the people of the equatorial forest region, this mask has an oval face and slightly heart-shaped horns.

About the Media

Because many African works of art were made from wood or other natural materials, they tended to decompose quickly in the humid, hot tropical climate of central Africa. Therefore, most traditional wooden African masks that can be found today are less than 200 years old. This mask was carved from a multicolored wood and might have been rubbed with palm oil to darken and preserve it.

About the Technique

Masks were carved from the wood of locally available trees. To shape the wood and create detail, sculptors used knives or an *adze*, which is a cutting tool with a thin, arched blade. Artists who created these masks often carved exaggerated, abstract features.

Mask

This interesting mask is among the most ancient Central American ceramic artifacts that have been found intact. This mask was created by an artist of the Tlatilco region in the Basin of Mexico, probably during the middle period of the pre-Christian epoch. Sculptors and potters of the ancient Tlatilco culture used delicate hand tools to give realistic features and animated facial expressions to their works of art.

▲ **Artist unknown.** (Tlatilco).
Mask. 12th–19th century B.C.
••
Ceramic pigment. 5$\frac{1}{4}$ inches (13.34 cm.) high.
The Metropolitan Museum of Art, New York, New York.

About Art History

The historic period during which Tlatilco ceramics were made, the first period of Meso-American art, is also known as the pre-classic period. During this time people in central Mexico were settling into central communities of farmers and hunters. Most of the terra-cotta Tlatilco artifacts seem to portray humans and animals, and this mask displays what appears to be primate-like features. Pre-classic artifacts that have been discovered in Mexico show that a focus was placed on form and balance in various types of ceramic pottery and sculpture.

About the Artwork

Masks from the ancient Mexican cultures of Olmec and Tlatilco varied from proportionate, lifelike human faces to more bizarre and monstrous creations, perhaps as representations of spiritual transformation. This ceramic mask, an exaggerated human or perhaps primate face, is too small to have been worn as a covering for the face and may have been intended as a part of a sculpture or a larger costume. The arching lines of the eyebrows,

eyes, ears, and mouth are a good example of Tlatilco attention to artwork's rhythm and form.

About the Media

The Basin of Mexico provided the early Tlatilco people with an abundance of mineral-rich clay soil with which to create many different functional and ceremonial objects. Kilns were designed and built after years of experimentation with primitive methods of baking clay, such as by carefully placing the clay pieces between layers of slow-burning wood in open fires. The exact method used to fire this mask is not known.

About the Technique

Formed by hand from clay, dried in the sun, painted, polished with a stone, and then fired, this mask is a classic example of ancient Mexican sculpture. Olmec and Tlatilco ceramics were usually original, one-of-a-kind pieces, because these cultures did not use molds to copy or mass-produce objects.

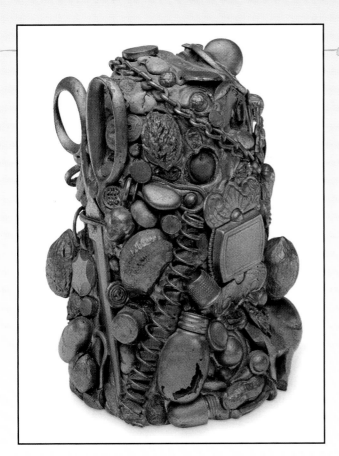

Memory Jar

This memory jar was made around the beginning of the twentieth century by an unknown artist. The artists who create sculptures like this come from many different ethnic groups and geographic regions, so it is difficult to determine the individual who made this particular piece.

◄ **Artist unknown.** (North America).
Memory Jar. c. 1925.

Mixed media. $8\frac{3}{10} \times 5\frac{1}{2}$ inches (21.07 × 14 cm.).
Museum of International Folk Art, Santa Fe, New Mexico.

About Art History

This memory jar is a type of artwork known as *recycled art.* Recycled art comes in countless forms, from simple vessels and collages similar to this memory jar to complex works in which recycled items have been creatively transformed into entirely new shapes. The creation of recycled art in America has evolved gradually. People have been reusing materials in the creation of housewares, clothing, furniture, and decorative items for centuries. During the Great Depression, farm women used empty sacks from animal feed to make curtains, bedding, and clothing for their families. Quilt makers use cloth scraps left over from other projects to sew beautiful, multicolored bedcovers and pillows.

About the Artwork

The intended purpose of this memory jar is a mystery to art historians. Several theories exist about its function or inspiration, including the idea that it may have been a kind of three-dimensional scrapbook for displaying some of its maker's favorite childhood items. Another theory is that this memory jar was made as a remembrance of a deceased loved one. It is also possible that it was made merely as a piece of decorative artwork for display in the artist's home or studio.

About the Media

This recycled-art memory vessel was made using a glass jar as a base. The jar was covered with a dough-like medium into which various found objects were pressed. The objects embedded in the vessel include a spring, a spoon, a thimble, a small mirror, a fish charm, nuts and bolts, and a pair of scissors.

About the Technique

Although the exact technique used to make this memory jar is not known, the dough medium was wrapped and pressed around the jar, and then the recycled objects were pressed into the soft dough before it hardened. It is possible that some of the items were glued onto the vessel's surface after the dough hardened.

Mother of the Eagles

The yarn painting, *Mother of the Eagles,* was made by an unknown artist of the Huichol Indians of Santa Catarina in Jalisco, Mexico. The Huichol Indians, a cultural and ethnic group descended from the Aztecs, live in the mountainous central Mexican states of Jalisco and Nayarit. Huichol artists do not sign their artwork, which makes it difficult to identify the artist who created a specific piece. Within local Huichol culture, however, community members can often determine an artist's identity by observing the style, materials, and workmanship of the piece.

▲ **Artist unknown.** (Huichol People, Mexico). *Mother of the Eagles.* 1991.

Braided yarn embedded in vegetable wax on wood.
$15\frac{3}{4} \times 19\frac{1}{2}$ inches (40 × 49.53 cm.). Private collection.

About Art History

The steep and rugged landscape and the dry conditions of the region where the Huichol live make subsistence farming difficult and risky. The Huichol have developed strong cultural traditions that center around praise and homage to the gods who are believed to control natural forces. Honoring the gods and asking them for favorable weather conditions and bountiful, healthy crops is the purpose of many rituals and celebrations in Huichol culture, and often Huichol artwork is made to please and celebrate the gods. Today there are about 18,000 Huichol.

About the Artwork

The images included in this yarn painting tell a story. In the center of the piece the mother of the eagles spreads her wings over three candles. It is believed that this yarn painting was made as an offering to the goddess to ask her for rain. The scene also shows two snakes descending from the sky, and zigzag lines that appear to be lightning bolts. These may symbolize rainstorms.

About the Media

Mother of the Eagles is made of colorful yarn, and vegetable wax on a thin, wooden backing.

About the Technique

The artist who created *Mother of the Eagles* braided thin strands of colorful yarn and then embedded the strands into vegetable wax, which served as an adhesive. The braided yarn was carefully arranged into parallel lines, both straight and curved. Strands were laid closely together to create a surface dense with color. Each figure in the scene has been perfectly outlined in a contrasting color, creating a well-defined shape. This yarn painting was created against a flat wooden background.

Navajo Blanket, Eye Dazzler

The Navajo people live in the Southwestern United States. They called themselves *Dineh,* "The People of the earth." In the early 1800s, the Navajo were a powerful and warring people. At that time, they were called "lords of the soil." In 1863, Colonel Kit Carson, commander of the first New Mexico Volunteers, defeated the Navajo people and forced them to relocate to Fort Sumner on the Pecos River in New Mexico. The Navajos were also forced to sign a peace treaty promising never to fight with U.S. settlers, Mexicans, or other Native Americans.

◀ **Artist unknown (Navajo)**. (United States). *Navajo Blanket, Eye Dazzler.* 1890.

Wool, cotton; tapestry weave; slit tapestry; dovetailed tapestry.
75 × 57 inches (190.5 × 144.78 cm.).
Dallas Museum of Art, Dallas, Texas. Textile Purchase Fund.

About Art History

The earliest surviving Navajo blankets date from the late 1700s and early 1800s. Most of the blankets were found in caves and remain only as fragments. The most important blanket fragments were found in the Cañon del Muerto, remembered in Navajo history as Massacre Cave because families were killed there by Spanish troops in 1805.

About the Artwork

The contrast between the earth tones of the diamond shapes creates a dizzying vibration. An additional shimmer is produced by the different patterns. The diamond-shaped patterns were created by using narrow bands of natural and dark yarns, thin, dyed strips, and sometimes unraveled yarns or other fabric materials.

About the Media

The Navajo used wool to create their blankets. They sheared sheep to gather wool for weaving. After shearing, the wool was shaken to remove sand and then placed on bushes. Women pulled out burrs and sticks by hand, then cleaned and untangled the wool. A simple wooden spindle was used to spin the wool.

About the Technique

Eye dazzler is a broad term for a style that developed with the introduction of chemical dyes made from coal tar products. This type of dye is known as *aniline* dye. Blankets containing aniline dye have been dated to the 1870s. The dyes became popular after 1880. Blankets of hand-spun and machine-spun yarns were used to create eye dazzlers.

Portrait of Yinxiang, the First Prince of Yi

The portrait was made by an unknown Chinese artist sometime during the Manchu Qing dynasty.

◄ **Artist unknown.** (China). *Portrait of Yinxiang, the First Prince of Yi.* 1686–1730.

Ink and color on silk. $73\frac{1}{2} \times 48$ inches (186.69 × 121.92 cm.). Arthur M. Sackler Gallery, Smithsonian Institution, Washington, D.C.

About Art History

The Qing dynasty was a time when China was ruled by the Manchu from Manchuria. The reigns of the first three Qing emperors marked a peaceful time, when education and the arts grew and flourished in China. Writing and the visual arts, including porcelain work and painting, are some of the art forms for which the Qing dynasty is best remembered.

About the Artwork

The silk painting *Portrait of Yinxiang, the First Prince of Yi* is a portrait of a Chinese prince dressed in his richly embroidered royal clothing, shoes, and hat. The pose in which the prince sits is the traditional body posture found in royal portraits of the Qing dynasty. Many of the paintings of royalty from this period show the subjects in this pose and wearing necklaces very similar to the one shown in this portrait. The composition of *Portrait of Yinxiang, the First Prince of Yi* is an example of how approximate symmetry is sometimes used in formal portraits.

About the Media

Winxiang, Prince Yi was made using silk cloth and natural pigments.

About the Technique

Portrait of Yinxiang, the First Prince of Yi was made by painting ink and vegetable pigments onto a flattened, stretched silk cloth. The silk may have been held taut within a frame during the painting process.

Sun Transformation Mask

This mask was made by Charlie James of the Kwakiutl peoples of northwestern Canada. The term *Kwakiutl* is used to refer collectively to approximately 5,500 tribes of the Canadian First Nations. Another term, *Kwakwaka'wakw,* is used by Kwakiutl peoples to describe themselves and their tribal affiliations with other members of the Kwakiutl.

◀ **Charlie James.** (Southern Kwakiutl).
Sun Transformation Mask. Early nineteenth century.
• •
Royal British Columbia Museum, British Columbia, Canada.

About Art History

Although Kwakiutl myths of ancestry vary from tribe to tribe, some supernatural beings are recurrent characters in the myths of all Kwakiutl tribes. The sun, a sky element, was one of the supernatural beings believed capable of removing its outer skin and becoming human for the purpose of creating a family lineage. In order to hide its human form, the sun being would wear a transformation mask and then change back into its supernatural form. Transformation masks were used in many different kinds of Kwakiutl ceremonies and special events, such as dances, theatrical performances, and heritage celebrations.

About the Artwork

The sun is a popular subject of Kwakiutl masks, sometimes taking the form of a human or bird head surrounded by spikes or rays. This work is an example of Kwakiutl mask making, displaying human and bird features, bold traditional colors, and a double row of sharply radiating shapes representing light rays. Sun transformation masks like this one are still used in Kwakiutl ceremonies and celebrations in coastal regions of northwestern Canada.

About the Media

Kwakiutl masks were often made from the wood and bark of red or yellow cedar. Paints were mixed only in a few traditional colors, and were used to enhance or emphasize the features of the carved wooden mask.

About the Technique

The Kwakiutl *Sun Transformation Mask* was carved from cedar wood. The mask was then painted using traditional colors. Kwakiutl masks often had deep arching grooves, geometric and organic shapes, and convex and concave curves sculpted into their surfaces, giving the masks exaggerated features and monstrous facial expressions.

Toy Banks

These banks were made by an unidentified Metepec artist from the state of México, located in central Mexico. Metepec is a small town on the outskirts of the large city Toluca. Metepec is home to many masters of ceramic art. Because the banks were not signed, it has been impossible to find the specific ceramic artist who made these pieces. It is estimated that the banks were made in the early twentieth century.

▲ **Artist unknown.** (Mexico).
Toy Banks. Twentieth century.
San Antonio Museum of Art, San Antonio, Texas.

About Art History

Ceramics and woodcarvings have been important art forms throughout Mexico for thousands of years. The abundance of naturally occurring clay and numerous species of hardwood trees have provided countless generations of artists with materials for making sculptures, carvings, pottery, tools, and many other functional, utilitarian, ceremonial, religious, and decorative objects.

About the Artwork

Ceramic artists in Metepec are known for their skill in creating beautiful clay sculptures such as the *arboles de la vida,* or trees of life, and Day of the Dead figures. Although the exact origin and history of these banks is not known, it may be assumed that they were made as gifts or to sell to retail buyers or visitors to the region.

About the Media

These toy banks were made from hand-molded clay and paint.

About the Technique

After being formed, sculpted, and detailed with small hand tools, these banks were allowed to dry. Metepec ceramic artists took great care to ensure that no air pockets or bubbles of water were embedded within their pieces because these imperfections would expand during firing and cause the ceramics to explode. Once dry, the pieces were fired in a kiln and painted. The final process was coating the finished piece in a glossy, protective glaze.